Body Shaping

Body Shaping

A Slim-Down, Shape-Up Guide to Conquering Your Body's Trouble Spots and Fat Zones

MICHAEL YESSIS, PH.D.
columnist, *Muscle & Fitness* Magazine
with Porter Shimer

RODALE PRESS, EMMAUS, PENNSYLVANIA

Library of Congress Cataloging-in-Publication Data
Yessis, Michael.
Body shaping : a slim-down, shape-up guide to conquering your
   body's trouble spots and fat zones / Michael Yessis, with Porter Shimer.
     p.   cm.
   Includes index.
   ISBN 0–87596–194–0 hardcover
   ISBN 0–87596–222–X paperback
   1. Reducing exercises.   2. Reducing.   I. Shimer, Porter.   II. Title.
RA781.6.Y47   1994
646.7 ' 5—dc20   93–38989
                                         CIP

Distributed in the book trade by St. Martin's Press

2 4 6 8 10 9 7 5 3 1 hardcover
    4 6 8 10 9 7 5   paperback

OUR MISSION

We publish books that empower people's lives.

RODALE ❀ BOOKS

Notice

This book is intended as a reference volume only, not as a medical manual. The information given here is designed to help you make informed decisions about weight control, exercise and health. It is not intended as a substitute for any treatment or program that may have been prescribed by your doctor. Before you embark on any exercise program or change your diet, we recommend you consult your physician.

CONTENTS

ACKNOWLEDGMENTS

Special thanks to Frank Weiman, my agent, who worked out the details to make the book a reality.

Marc Patterson, director of marketing for Keiser Sports Health Equipment in Fresno, California, for his cooperation in providing many of the exercise machines shown.

Budd Coates for use of the Rodale Energy Center exercise facility for a number of photo sessions and Stan Green, associate art director, for his masterful role in coordinating the photo sessions. Stan also created the cover and interior design.

Roger Cloyd, vice president of Hoist Fitness Systems, who rushed through the new model of the glute-ham developer and made it ready for the book.

Paula Mintzer, athlete, professional model and "real mom," who embodies the Body Shaping principles. Paula runs, mountain-bikes, skis, participates in aerobics and competes in triathlons, plus she and her husband have a 4½-year-old daughter.

Edie Evans-Yessis, my understanding wife, who acted as a sounding board for many of my ideas.

Marissa Yessis, my daughter, for being such a great sport in posing for the initial photographs to demonstrate the various exercises.

Additional credit goes to Jacqueline Ann Burg, stylist; Mitch Mandel, photographer; Karen Kuchar, illustrator; and Sandy Freeman, interior layout designer.

Last, but not least, my deepest appreciation to Sharon Faelten, managing editor of health and fitness books at Rodale Press, who worked so diligently with me in shaping many of the key chapters.

FYI: The exercise apparel pictured in the Body Shaping workouts is from Body Wrappers, Nike and Softouch by Susan Fixel. The ankle weights are by All Pro Exercise Products, Jericho, New York. The dumbbells are by York Barbell Company, York, Pennsylvania. All free weights and workout benches were supplied by Lehigh Fitness Products, Emmaus, Pennsylvania. In addition to the Keiser machines, a number of Cybex machines appear throughout.

CHAPTER 1

THE BODY SHAPING PROMISE

A trimming and toning program that works with your body

Hello, and congratulations. By picking up this book, you've taken a giant step toward improving not just your appearance but your health, your happiness and the rest of your life. You'll need to take several more steps, of course. But in many ways, this first step is the most important (and perhaps the hardest).

Why?

Because you've accepted the responsibility. Part of you has come to realize that no one is more in control of your destiny—physically or emotionally—than you are. Just as you ultimately determine the type of work you do, the company you keep and the clothes you wear, you can *also* shed unwanted pounds and tone up bother-some areas, by changing what you eat and how you live your life.

In fact, food and exercise—two highly controllable factors—play a more significant role in how you look and feel than you might realize.

A nice idea, you say, but wishful thinking? You've got a family tree with such heavy "limbs" that it's ready to topple over? I can hear it now: "If I'd been able to choose some leaner ancestors, I wouldn't need this book in the first place."

For the good news, read on.

RECLAIMING YOUR RIGHT TO A BETTER BODY

Research now shows that heredity plays a relatively minor role in determining body shape, and how you deal with your heredity has a big influence on how you look. Let's cut to the chase: Data on twins, plus family studies, indicate that only about 25 percent of the body fat you carry is genetically determined at conception. Once you're born, a number of other factors (such as what you eat and how much you eat) take effect.

Where your body fat tends to collect—hips, abdomen, legs—is also partly due to hereditary and mostly due to your lifestyle, including your eating and exercise habits, and varies from person to person. But in general, body shape is roughly 50 percent genetic and 50 percent a factor of influences such as diet and exercise.

A noteworthy study on identical twins, presented to the American College of Sports Medicine some years ago, bears this out. Joseph Keul, of the Department of Human Performance Physiology and Sports Medicine at the University of Freiburg, in Germany, studied the effect different kinds of training had on two brothers. Both started life with the same physique—same number of muscles, same size. As adults, one became an endurance runner, one a strength trainer. The endurance runner had a higher heart volume and VO_2max (standard measures of aerobic fitness) than his brother. In addition, the endurance runner weighed approximately 35 pounds less than his brother.

But *how* these twins carried their weight also differed markedly. Photos published in *Medicine and Science in Sports Medicine* show that the brother who concentrated on weight training had broad shoulders and a narrow waist and was very well muscled. Despite his weight, in no way could he be considered fat or out of shape.

In comparison, the endurance runner was more evenly proportioned, with smaller muscles. From the neck down, you'd never guess they were twins.

The moral of the story is, you *can* alter what you were born with, for better or worse.

Lest you doubt that such dramatic alterations are possible for women, I've personally seen a number of cases where sisters looked dramatically different, largely due to differences in exercise and eating habits.

EXERCISE *IS* FEMININE

Since establishing the Sports Training Center in Escondido, California, in 1983, I've worked with 1,000 men and women. One of the reasons a lot of women get out of shape when they hit adulthood is poor exercise habits during childhood. (A lot of men fall into this category, too, of course.) A fair number of women today grew up playing house while the boys played sports. A generation ago, girls weren't encouraged to play softball, soccer, basketball or other sports. So they spent a lot less time running, jumping or doing other vigorous activities.

Even today, if you watch children at play, you'll see groups of girls sitting around talking while the boys play tag and get into fights. At a pool, the girls tend to congregate on the sidelines while the boys raise a ruckus in the water.

I'm not trying to perpetuate a stereotype or advocate physical conflict. The point is, people of either sex stand a better chance of successfully integrating exercise into their life if they're *conditioned* to see exercise as a normal part of their life. And that goes for girls as well as boys.

Luckily, athletic women are no longer considered unladylike. In fact, the women who have the best figures often turn out to be sports enthusiasts of some kind. Activities such as cycling, tennis and weight training help them maintain their shape.

JUST HOW MUCH CAN YOU EXPECT TO CHANGE?

Obviously, if you're five feet two inches tall and 35 years old, you can't do much about your height or age. You'll never be five-five, and you'll never be 30 years old again, either. Genes *do* determine your maximum height and other physical traits. But genes do *not* necessarily determine your *present* shape and fitness level. Just as changes in diet and lifestyle can

improve your blood pressure, cholesterol level and other internal physical traits, so can they remold your outer appearance. You may assume that you inherited your physique from your mother or dad. Or you'll never look like your beautiful older sister. But until now, maybe you haven't done everything you can do to change your proportions.

So take heart: Your body is a mound of "clay" just waiting to be "molded" far more than you may know. Depending on the muscles you exercise, how much weight you lift in your workouts and the number of repetitions you do of each exercise, you can selectively reproportion your given shape quite dramatically. Lots of repetitions with light weights tends to slim and tighten a particular body area, while fewer repetitions with heavier weights builds muscle and gives size. Thus, you can "add" here and "subtract" there to tone up trouble spots and produce a more desirable silhouette.

Add some aerobic exercise to your routine, moreover, and make the healthful changes in your diet that I'll be recommending in the pages ahead, and you can eliminate unwanted fat from your body and hence help accentuate your new shape even more.

Oh, and by the way: Don't worry that weight training will leave you looking like a female Arnold Schwarzenegger. While a few women develop exaggerated musculature, that's usually due to a genetic tendency toward male-pattern muscle mass, extremely intense workout regimens or use of artificial steroids (or some combination thereof). Most women will develop only to the point of looking well toned and "naturally enhanced."

TIME: YOU'VE GOT MORE THAN YOU THINK

I'm fully aware that women are under heavy time constraints, trying to manage at work, run a household smoothly, raise children and meet other obligations. We all have exactly 24 hours a day—no more, no less—and the day fills up pretty quickly. But by improving how you spend your time, you can find time for the things that are important to you (such as the toning workouts and fat-burning exercises that make up the Body Shaping plan).

As stress researcher Emmett E. Miller, M.D., of Menlo Park, California, explains, many people find themselves so busy with things that are urgent that they don't have time for things that are important.

There *is* a difference. Your day may be filled with tasks that demand attention and effort—right now. If you're like most women I know, you may feel pulled in seven different directions. But if sculpting a new body is important to you—and I assume it is, if you're reading this book—it's up to

you to make your workouts a priority and ignore, postpone or delegate tasks that sound urgent but aren't important and that get in the way of achieving your goal. You're *entitled* to stake out some time for yourself.

Another way to find time to work out is to analyze how you spend your leisure time. According to fitness scientist David C. Nieman, D.H.Sc., of Appalachian State University in Boone, North Carolina, the average American has 15 to 18 hours of leisure a week. At the same time, in most households, the television is on an average of 7 hours a day. For many, lack of desire, not lack of time, is the real obstacle to regular exercise. Once you have the desire, you'll find the time.

Another notion that stands in the way of regular exercise is that just because a woman leads a busy life—getting the kids off to school, commuting to work, doing errands and laundry and grocery shopping—she doesn't really need to exercise. But that's not so. The evidence is clear: If you want to reap the benefits, you need to average 20 to 30 minutes of exercise several days a week.

The payoff is, once you start to exercise, you'll increase your productivity by *20 percent or more*. Even people with demanding careers report that they experience enhanced mental energy and physical stamina, enabling them to accomplish in 40 hours what they used to do in 50. So you end up with 6 or 7 hours of free time a week!

ENJOY THE JOURNEY AS MUCH AS THE ARRIVAL

Chances are you've been on a "diet" at some time or another. Like a lot of people, you probably did everything exactly right—for the first month. Then you reverted to your normal eating habits, and you regained the weight you lost (and then some). That's because historically, most diets are too rigid. No one can stick with them for more than a few weeks. So the results are short-lived.

In my experience, the key to success in making the kinds of diet and exercise changes described in this book is to look beyond immediate goals—thinner thighs, a fuller bosom, slimmer hips or whatever other goal you may have. *Enjoy* the process, so recreational exercise becomes natural and automatic. Likewise, I'm confident you'll quickly learn to savor the foods in the eating plan described in chapter 14—high in a variety of slimming complex carbohydrates and low in fat-building, energy-draining foods.

Think beyond changing one or two isolated behaviors or one or two isolated trouble spots. Instead, look at Body Shaping as a matter of reshaping your life as well. That's the key.

BE PREPARED TO GO SLOWLY

I strongly encourage you not to try to go too fast in your Body Shaping quest. Yes, set goals and work diligently toward them. But what's more important is the overall direction in which you're heading. When you commit to the Body Shaping program, you're not just changing your body, you're improving your life.

Case in point: I remember working with a woman named Susan a few years ago who, like many women, was unhappy with her body and wanted to see results overnight. Susan had devoted the last 18 years to raising her children and had put on 50 pounds. She had lost considerable muscle tone and was determined to make up for lost time.

Susan started doing light aerobics. That helped a little. But she wasn't satisfied with her progress.

When she came to the Sports Training Center for help, I was frank but diplomatic.

"You can't expect to rebuild Rome in a day," I told her. "It's taken you years to fall as out of shape as you are now. So it's going to take at least a few months even to begin to turn that collapse around."

First of all, I asked Susan about her diet and recommended some changes. I also recommended certain resistance exercises—to tone up her trouble spots—and a program of aerobic exercise to burn off the extra pounds.

After one year, Susan lost 35 pounds, regained most of her muscle tone, lost *six inches* off her waist and trimmed her hips and thighs. What's more, she felt like a new woman and was amazed at how much more energy she had. Susan planned her day around her workouts, not the other way around. And she truly enjoyed the activities she pursued.

Susan still had a few more pounds to lose and a little more remodeling to do on her body. But she accepted her goals as long-term ones and was satisfied with her new body—satisfied enough to stick with it.

When I last saw Susan, she was overjoyed. She told me she looks better now than she did in her teens and twenties!

This book is peppered with success stories like Susan's. With the workouts in this book, you, too, can be a new woman.

CHAPTER 2

❖

MUSCLE,
THE MISSING LINK
Making the most of a natural resource

So far, we've seen that your physique, stubborn though it may seem, has not been carved in any sort of genetic stone. If you want to make changes in your figure badly enough— and I'm talking about major changes— you can. True, you can't change your basic bone structure. But you can change the flesh (that is, muscle and fat) responsible for giving that structure its shape. As I suggested in chapter 1, it might help to think of your body as a mound of clay waiting to be sculpted. With the right exercises and dietary habits, you can, to a large degree, carve out just about whatever figure you desire.

You needn't become a fitness slave to sculpt your muscle. The secret, as

we'll be seeing, lies not so much in working hard as in working *smart*— knowing the right exercises to do in the right ways with the right frequency and intensity for the right body parts. Your body will take care of the rest.

"Nice idea," you say, but you have your doubts? You've tried exercise programs only to run out of steam before achieving any appreciable results?

Maybe the reason you ran out of steam was that you weren't working closely enough with your body's basic physiology. There's been a link missing in most of the fitness and figure control programs I've seen women pursue. That missing link has been resistance training (that is, weight training or strength training). Very few

7

of these programs have realized how important resistance training is for achieving the fitness goals most women seek. The slimness you want, the firmness, the shapeliness, the energy, the stamina, the improved health and ability to handle stress—they're all waiting for you once you begin to develop your body's natural, yet for most women untapped, strength.

THE PHYSIOLOGY OF MUSCLE

To fully appreciate the pivotal role of muscle toning in Body Shaping, it helps to get a clear picture of exactly what muscle tissue looks like, how it functions and, most importantly, how muscles are affected by the dynamics of resistance training, aerobics and changes in diet.

You probably learned in your high school biology class that the body has not one but three kinds of muscle—smooth muscle (lining the walls of the stomach and other vital organs); striated, or skeletal, muscle (which works your legs, hips, arms, back, neck and so forth); and heart muscle (which is a combination of both).

Skeletal muscle also holds you upright. And since muscles make up approximately 45 percent of your body weight, they give your body shape—so they're instrumental in toning and shaping your contours.

All totaled, you have 434 muscles in your body. But don't worry, you don't have to work *all* of them to get in shape. Only 150 or so (75 pairs) are involved in posture and motion. Body Shaping exercises target the seven major muscle groups—the chest, the shoulders and back, the arms, the waist (abdomen and lower back), the hips and buttocks, the thighs and the calves and ankles—the trouble zones that people most often want to reshape.

If you were to examine skeletal muscle under a microscope, you'd notice many cells combined into long, slender muscle fibers (myofibrils), some of which are almost a foot long and a hair's width in diameter. Bundles of 150 or so of these slender fibers are held together with connective tissue to form muscles such as the triceps (at the back of your upper arms), the gluteus maximus (in the buttocks) and the quadriceps femoris (at the front of your thighs).

Muscles are crafted into different shapes, depending on their place and function. The biceps (in your arms) are spindle-shaped, the pectoral muscles (in the chest) are fan-shaped, and the trapezius (in your back) is flat and sheetlike.

As you work through your Body Shaping routine, bear in mind that muscles contain two kinds of fiber. White, fast-twitch muscles, which are usually the larger of the two, are most efficient at explosive efforts of speed or strength—such as lifting a heavy weight very quickly. Red, slow-twitch fibers are built for the long haul—they're used mainly in endurance efforts such as long-distance running. Almost all activities, however, use both.

As with stature and other inherited physical traits, people vary in their proportion of fast-twitch and slow-twitch fibers. If experience has shown that you're best at short sprints and quick bursts of energy, most likely you have a predominance of white, fast-twitch fibers. If you can run long distances with relative ease, you probably have more red, slow-twitch fibers. (Here's a bit of fitness trivia you can use to impress people: Studies done on elite athletes have shown that world-class sprinters can have up to 90 percent white, fast-twitch fibers, while marathon runners have up to 90 percent red, slow-twitch fibers.)

All that is academic, though: You don't need to worry about what kind of muscle fibers predominate. In any given muscle contraction—whether you're doing leg lifts or using a slideboard—both fast-twitch and slow-twitch muscle fibers are involved. For the muscle to become well developed, both fibers must be developed. It follows that to become well shaped and toned, you need to do both anaerobic efforts (such as strength training) to target mainly the white fibers and aerobic training (such as tennis) that uses mainly the red fibers.

Strength training is the easiest and most effective way to develop muscle.

Aerobics (described in detail in chapter 3) helps your Body Shaping program in other ways. Aerobics alone may leave you thinner—with smaller muscles—but it won't tone. Combining strength training with aerobics also encourages growth of small arterioles, feeder veins that deliver oxygen, glycogen and other nutrients to muscles, adding to the toning effect.

MUSCLES NEED REST TO WORK BEST

Understanding muscle physiology also helps you understand why you may feel a little sore after working out with weights—and why you should skip a day between strength-training workouts. The more intensely you work out, the longer it takes for muscles to refuel and repair microscopic tears in the fiber that occur naturally. Generally, however, the large muscles of the body, such as those in the chest, back and thighs, need anywhere from 24 to 48 hours to recover. The smaller muscles, such as those in the shins and forearms, take up to 24 hours.

Exactly how much time your muscles will need to recover from strength-training sessions will depend on your fitness level, how intensely you work out and how well nourished your muscles are. But in general, during a weight-training workout, the muscles can partially recover within a minute or so—enough to give you ample energy to go on to the next exercise or set. By the end of a workout, you should feel somewhat fatigued for an hour or so, especially if you've been working out for a month or two. Be sure to follow the appropriate recommended workloads for each exercise and progress *gradually.*

It's also worth noting that a well-nourished muscle will recover and develop more effectively than a poorly nourished muscle. So paying attention to your diet (the third prong in the Body Shaping program, along with aerobic exercise and strength training) is part of the plan.

Saunas, hydrotherapy (such as spas or even a shower or a warm bath) and massage can speed recovery, too. So can a light workout on the day following a particularly enthusiastic workout. Both heat and light exercise increase circulation, delivering nutrients for necessary repair and carting away waste products generated through muscular effort.

So allow for a complete recovery—a day or more—once a week. Otherwise, you could end up overtraining, which could set you back greatly.

MORE LEAN MUSCLE, LESS FAT

At this point, you're probably wondering how developing and toning your muscles help you deal with unwanted fat. Again, it's simple physiology. Muscle tissue is the best fat-burning tissue your body has. What's more, as you get into better and better

shape, your muscles get even better at burning fat. Because the more you use a muscle, the more nourishment and energy—and hence calories—it needs in order to restore and replenish itself from the demands of exercise (a phenomenon known as recovery or adaptation).

Your body does not merely replace what has been used up, however. Your body reacts to the depleted stores by undergoing changes that allow you to do even more the next time you work out. This is known as supercompensation, a phenomenon that allows you to develop not only more energy but strength and greater aerobic fitness.

To understand this better, think of your present energy level, muscle tone, aerobic fitness or body shape as a baseline. When you work out, the body uses up your energy supply (the depletion phase). During rest and as you sleep, the body recovers and replenishes the energy supply that has been used.

However, because the body does not like these depleted states, it maintains additional energy supplies at the "work sites"—your muscles. As a result, your base level increases. In essence, the body restructures itself to allow it to perform on this higher level.

The metabolic activity and associated caloric costs can be quite considerable. Strenuous muscular effort can boost the rate at which a fit, well-toned muscle burns calories by as much as a whopping 20-fold. In other words, how intensely you work, and for how long, determines your muscles' "appetite" for calories. You win both ways—during and after.

With Body Shaping, you'll become stronger, firmer and more shapely but not *over*muscled. And you will not wind up looking like Hulk Hogan in the process. Female bodybuilders who develop massive muscles devote their entire lives to looking the way they do, working at levels that are far more intense than what you will be doing in this program, taking muscle development to the limit and achieving near-impossible body fat levels of 5 to 10 percent. Regrettably, many take dangerous, muscle-building steroids to boost their levels of male hormones, both to develop bigger muscles and to work at that level.

No, the muscle you do develop will be purely by your own choice and design. If you decide you'd like more prominent breasts, for example, you can have them by adding some muscular bulk and firmness to the pectoral muscles that lie beneath the breasts. Or if you'd like slightly wider shoulders to help compensate for a wide waist, or more "outstanding" buttocks, or shapelier calves, you can have them.

That's the beauty of strength training and my Body Shaping system: You can target just about any area of your body you wish. Depending on how much weight you lift, and the number of repetitions you perform, you can begin to tailor your physique, adding size to areas you may feel are too small and slimming down areas you may feel are too large. It comes down to two guiding principles.

• Fewer repetitions with heavier weights enhance size where needed.

• More repetitions with lighter weights tone and slim, for a leaner look.

Together, these two principles enable you to sculpt out just about whatever figure you desire. There are certain genetic limitations to what you can achieve, of course, given your basic bone structure and body type as we discussed in chapter 1, but I must say that I've seen some remarkable shapes achieved even by women who had practically no shape.

WEIGHTS PLUS AEROBICS FOR WELL-TONED CONTOURS

Aerobic exercise—the cardiovascular kind that's good for your heart and lungs—is the second "prong" of the Body Shaping program. By toning, strengthening and, in some cases, enlarging certain muscles through strength training, you'll be achieving most of the basic muscular shape that you want. But it's with the additional help of aerobic exercise that you'll be burning even more calories and hence helping reduce fat that could be hiding that shape from view.

To understand how this works, picture a steak (a cut of meat not unlike your own anatomy). Essentially, you're looking at muscle. In and around the steak is fat. In fact, the fat in beef—marbling—is what makes a good steak so tender. Similarly, fat is what gives you smooth, rounded hips, thighs and so forth.

The ratio of muscle to fat carried on your frame has a clear bearing on how you look and how fit you are. The higher the percentage of muscle, the better proportioned you are, and the fitter you are. The higher the percentage of fat, the more out of shape you are (figuratively *and* literally).

Your muscles are *designed* for exertion. If you lead a sedentary life—get very little exercise—your muscles will shrink (the myofibrils dissolve). If you increase your food consumption *and* don't exercise, you will become fatter. An interesting study conducted by Ellington Darden, Ph.D., director of research for Nautilus Sports/Medicine Industries in Gainesville, Florida, tracked 1,000 women over the course of many years. His observations are startling: At age 14, the average

---

TAMING YOUR TROUBLE SPOTS AND FAT ZONES

A unique study conducted by researchers at Oregon State University measured decade-by-decade gain in percentage of body fat (and corresponding loss of lean muscle) in 233 women between the ages of 20 and 78. The results show that some areas gain fat more readily than others. Luckily, it's never too late to slow these age-related changes, with a conscientious Body Shaping program of diet and exercise.

Measurement	20s-30s	30s-40s	40s-50s	50s-60s	60s-70s
Arm fat (%)	+7.2	+10.0	+8.0	+7.4	+1.0
Arm lean (kg)	−0.5	−8.0	−2.6	−1.1	−1.6
Leg fat (%)	+8.8	+10.9	+10.5	+1.7	+4.5
Leg lean (kg)	−5.4	−6.8	−6.4	−1.1	−1.6
Trunk fat (%)	+8.3	+14.1	+13.0	+10.7	+0.9
Trunk lean (kg)	No change	No change	No change	No change	No change
Whole body fat (%)	+7.1	+11.5	+11.0	+5.2	+2.7
Whole body lean (kg)	−1.9	−4.0	−3.5	−3.3	−2.8

SOURCE: "Regional and Whole Body Tissue Composition Changes with Age in Adult Females," C. Harris et al, *Medicine and Science in Sports and Exercise,* supplement to vol. 25, no. 5, May 1993, p. S101.

woman weighs 120 pounds, 48 of which are muscle and 20 of which are fat. Her percentage of body fat is a little over 16 percent.

By age 30, the average woman has reached 136 pounds. In the process, she's lost 8 pounds of muscle and more than *doubled* her fat, to 44 pounds (a little more than 32 percent fat). By age 40 or 50, as the total fat and pounds creep up, muscle continues to disappear at the rate of ½ pound a year. (A more recent study by other researchers, shown in the table on the opposite page, shows similar patterns.)

Exercise and diet can change the muscle-to-fat ratio in your favor.

• If you eat the same amount of fat, protein and carbohydrates, strength-train and do aerobics, you may build muscle and decrease body fat levels, changing your shape.

• If you eat less fat and exercise, you increase muscle and lose fat.

• If you exercise aerobically but do not change your diet, you will also lose fat (but you won't build muscle).

Combining both resistance training and aerobics can achieve the best results, proof of which has been demonstrated in some convincing research. In one study, conducted at the South Shore YMCA in Quincy, Massachusetts, 72 men and women were divided into two groups. One engaged in aerobic activity for 30 minutes, three times a week; the other divided its workouts between 15 minutes of aerobics and

15 minutes of strength training. Both groups ate identical diets consisting of 60 percent carbohydrates, 20 percent protein and 20 percent fat.

Eight weeks later, the group that combined aerobics with weight training lost substantially more fat than the aerobics-only group, dropping an average of 10 pounds of fat per person compared with only 3 pounds for the aerobics group. More importantly, the people in the weights-plus-aerobics group gained more muscle as well—an average of 2 pounds per person. In contrast, the aerobics group had actually lost some muscle.

Granted, this is only one study, but it provides a strong argument, nonetheless, that the best way to make substantial improvements in your physique is to cash in on the benefits of strength training for building muscle and strength training plus aerobics for burning calories *and* fat. (As stated elsewhere, aerobic exercise can do very little to build muscle—hence the need for a combination of the two for achieving your most dramatic and desirable Body Shaping results.)

THE STORY OF HELEN

I recall one woman in particular who is a classic example of how muscle toning plus aerobics builds a great body.

Helen was narrow in the shoulders but wide through the buttocks and hips. To minimize her pear-shaped appearance, Helen did muscle-building exercises to slightly broaden the deltoid muscles of her shoulders. I also had her do muscle-toning exercises to firm up the muscles of her hips and waist. *And* I advised her to take up a walking program to help her burn fat from all over.

The results were quite remarkable. Even though Helen had lost "only" two inches from her waist, it looked like quite a bit more, since she had added an inch to the width of her shoulders. This "addition/subtraction" technique—using strength training to add muscle to where you feel you may be too small, combined with toning exercises plus aerobics to reduce where you feel you may be too large—is the backbone of the Body Shaping system.

And by the way, don't worry that if you stop working out for any reason, your newly developed muscle will turn to fat. Fat and muscle are two completely different substances and aren't interchangeable. Comparing fat to muscle is like comparing oranges to grapefruit—related, but distinctly different.

OTHER BENEFITS OF THE BODY SHAPING PROGRAM

The work you do to selectively re-proportion your body benefits more than just your waistline. There are other advantages to feeling fit and trim—improved self-esteem that carries over to your job, relationships and general outlook. People who work out find that they tend to:

Gain greater self-confidence.

As a fitness consultant, I find it very rewarding to see the gains in self-confidence that occur when women begin to work out. Many are amazed at their own capabilities. Some thought they'd never be able to lose the excess weight that was hiding their waist, clinging to their hips or otherwise discouraging them. Seeing the changes in their appearance, getting stronger and improving their overall fitness give them newfound confidence. Now they look better—and they know it! Once they see that they can handle the weights and do the exercises, they have the confidence to accomplish other tasks that they thought were impossible.

I recall one woman in a class I taught, a required course in beginner swimming. The semester goal was to swim one mile without stopping. This young woman had difficulty learning the various strokes and didn't pick up the skill very quickly. Since it was a required course, however, she practiced every day. I'd never seen anyone put in so much time and effort to get through the class. As you can probably guess, she improved—and she swam the mile. She was so elated, she thanked me over and over again. By tackling this one goal, she overcame what she thought was a lack of ability to achieve what she assumed was an impossible goal. She knew she had an obstacle to overcome, and she did it. With this victory, she felt able to conquer any problem that arose. Getting involved in an exercise program could instill similar self-confidence in anyone.

Improve self-esteem and feel a greater sense of satisfaction. Why do something if it's hard? Because of the end results. Think about it: Before you can truly derive satisfaction (and other benefits) from an activity, you have to go through a learning period. You lift a weight a certain number of times, in a certain way, to work a particular muscle to reshape a particular muscle group. The result is a very satisfying experience. You start to like it—and you like yourself better for persevering and reaching the ultimate goal. With that comes an inner reward, the pleasure that sends you back for more. When the workout is over, you'll like yourself for doing it.

Enjoy more energy than ever. Almost all the women who start a weight and exercise program comment that they have more energy. This may come as a surprise at first. After all, exercise uses energy stores. But during rest (and especially at night, when you're asleep), the body regenerates to renew energy that's been used. It does this very efficiently—too efficiently, in fact. Not only does the body renew, but also it raises your energy level. However, it soon returns to normal, even though you're working harder. (As you work out more, you might also notice an increase in appetite—a perfectly natural response to this heightened state of energy. Just be sure you eat nutritious foods with high biological value and not rich, high-calorie sweets, greasy snacks or baked goods, to avoid weight gain.)

In any case, as you become stronger, you'll find it easier to do everything from climbing stairs to washing the dog, the result being that you'll feel noticeably more energetic. Many women tell me they have far more energy for virtually everything they do, thanks to the boost in "horse-power" they gain from their workouts. Some research suggests that improved fitness levels may even help combat chronic fatigue immune dysfunction syndrome, a perplexing condition that some say is reaching near epidemic proportions.

Feel more at ease. Another important benefit of muscular activity is the release of emotional tension. Exercise is a great way to release muscle tension caused by worry and other taxing emotions. Many women find that muscular exercise offers a satisfying emotional outlet; for others, it provides a channel for self-expression and creativity or a sense of achievement. If you've never experienced the feeling associated with well-toned muscles, you're in store for a treat.

A number of studies have found that working out also releases anxiety. Part of the reason is simple distraction. Say you're playing a sport—tennis, for example. You have to concentrate on the ball, figure out where to hit it, anticipate the return and so forth. Your mind is occupied with succeeding at the game. Afterward, a problem that may have worried you beforehand doesn't seem so major after all.

There's something about strength training in particular that seems to decrease anxiety. One study found that anxiety levels in people who worked out went down and stayed down as they went about their daily business. In comparison, anxiety levels in people who performed the same daily activities but didn't work out were higher. This is important, because after resistance training, it's normal for blood pressure to increase slightly, and high blood pressure is often associated with anxiety. Even though blood pressure went up slightly and remained higher for up to two hours in the people who worked out, they were still less anxious.

Handle stress better. Working with weights does more than relieve anxiety. It helps you adapt to stress. As you get stronger, you'll notice that your muscles release tension more easily. When you feel more at ease, your body systems will function more efficiently, cutting your risk of stress-associated conditions such as heart attacks and ulcers. (Researchers speculate that anger and hostility, two emotions frequently triggered in high-stress situations, contribute to heart disease by triggering the release of cortisol and other adrenaline-like hormones that, in excess, are harmful.)

What's more, you feel capable of just about anything. Part of this comes from gains in physical strength. But part of it comes from your new sense of confidence. Think of this as developing mental toughness along with physical toughness. When a problem arises, you feel you can conquer it without undue stress.

Reduce stress while trimming the waistline. A fascinating study by psychologists Mareille Rebuffe-Scrive, Ph.D., and Judith Rodin, Ph.D., of Yale University in New Haven, Connecticut, found that the psychological stress people can't handle tends to augment the deposit of fat on the abdomen. The link, it appears, is cortisol, a hormone released when the body is under stress. In some people, a sudden flood of cortisol, unleashed when you're under pressure, diverts body fat stores to the torso as part of the fight-or-flight response. The culprit, according to the authors, is a lower coping ability. So exercise helps you trim your waistline *two* ways—by melting tummy fat *and* by helping you cope with stress.

Sleep more restfully. Your workouts should leave you mildly and pleasantly fatigued by the end of the day, helping you fall asleep quickly. Once you get your strength and energy levels up, moreover, you're also likely to enjoy deeper and more restful sleep, thus boosting your energy levels during the day even more. This is because your body will be needing high-quality sleep to recuperate from your workouts. Many of the women I've helped train tell me they now fall asleep in just a few minutes, whereas it would sometimes take them agonizing hours before.

Stand straight and tall. Good posture is essential to looking good. But it's also a sign of pride in your appearance and your achievements—and it allows your heart, lungs and digestive system to function properly. If you slouch, for example, with your hips tilted forward and your abdomen protruding, you compress the rib cage, preventing the lungs from expanding fully. Accentuating the curvature of the spine in this way also pinches spinal nerves and causes back pain.

To maintain effective posture, not only when standing but also when you're seated or playing sports, you need strong muscles. To hold your body erect, for example, you need powerful back muscles. To keep your pelvis properly aligned when seated, you need support from your hip and back muscles. So by building up your muscles, the Body Shaping exercises also improve your posture.

Balance well. Without good balance, it becomes very difficult to perform the kinds of aerobic activities you need to burn body fat and perform the Body Shaping exercises. Balance is dynamic, an ongoing series of barely perceptible corrections involving the constant contraction and relaxation of

muscles. The stronger you are, and the more muscular control you have, the better your balance will be. This becomes increasingly important as women reach middle age and beyond, since studies show that poor balance, not weak muscles, is responsible for fractures such as broken hips in many older women.

Reduce risk of injury. Stronger muscles enable you to withstand the stresses and strains of physical activity. If your muscles are weak, stress is placed on the tendons. If the tendons are weak, stress then falls on the ligaments. If the ligaments are stretched, they stay stretched, leaving joints loose and prone to injury. If a ligament tears, surgery may be necessary to repair it.

The higher your level of participation in sports, be it running, racquetball or whatever, the more protection you need from injury. So the more active your lifestyle, the stronger your muscles need to be. As the years go on, you'll be able to continue to do everything you enjoy—gardening, cycling and so forth—without being hobbled or laid up by injuries.

I remember a young woman—a ski racer—who had very loose shoulder ligaments. Her shoulder dislocated during a race, after a pole plant. Yet for racing, a vigorous pole plant is important. She was scheduled for surgery. I suggested a strength-training program instead, and that did the trick. I devised a program of workouts that emphasized the action used in skiing to strengthen her shoulders. After performing the exercises vigorously for six months, she began the racing season with no problems. But she has to maintain her strength; otherwise, the shoulder muscles would become weak again, and the joint would slip.

Succeed at sports (and have more fun). The stronger your muscles become, the faster you can run down a tennis ball, power a serve and hit through on a golf swing. Most sports require strength as much as they require coordination, so by toning your muscles, you'll be better at whatever recreational activities you choose to pursue. One woman here at the Sports Training Center, an avid golfer, has been able to lower her handicap by five strokes since beginning to work out. "I'm now a good 20 yards farther off the tee," she recently told me.

It's worth mentioning that at times, sports are played for business as well as recreation. Many women, for example, are now taking up golf so that they can network on the links along with male associates. So enhancing your ability to play may enhance your career!

Have healthier children. One of the biggest complaints I hear from women is "Look how out of shape I am since I've had children." Or "It took me two years to get back in shape after I had my first child; now I'm having another. Am I going to be in even worse shape this time?"

Working out *before* you get pregnant can help you get back in shape quickly afterward. What's more, you'll have an easier pregnancy. My wife did extensive back and other midsection exercises before having our daughter. She never experienced any lower back pain whatsoever during her entire pregnancy. Yet if you talk to any women about to bear children, most will complain of back problems.

If you work out, your baby will be better off, too. Studies of female athletes show that their babies usually are bigger, healthier and stronger than the newborns of sedentary mothers and that athletic mothers tend to regain their pre-pregnancy figures faster than inactive moms. Add the good example that physically fit mothers tend to set for their children, and you have yet another reason why good fitness makes good sense within the family context. Fitness can become a family "trait" children feel inspired to live up to, plus doing fitness activities together as a family can help promote the kind of communication and emotional closeness that can last a lifetime.

Ease painful menstruation. Research now indicates that muscular exertion may help alleviate some of the discomforts associated with heavy menstrual flow. The reasons can be psychological or physical—or possibly a combination of both. The production of natural pain-fighting chemicals called endorphins could be involved, and/or the ability of exercise to reduce tension and imbue good feelings of accomplishment could also be at play.

Age more slowly. Studies show that people who are athletic not only live longer, they lead more active lives as well. Women in their twenties and thirties who remain active into their seventies tend to maintain their youthful looks and figures—and don't have to look into cosmetic surgery when they hit age 50 or 60. In fact, some women become *more* active as they leave the responsibilities of child care behind.

An active Body Shaping fitness program can afford women the protection against heart disease they need after menopause while giving them the stamina of women half their age. In one study, Christine Wells, Ph.D., professor of exercise science at Arizona State University in Tempe, found that women masters runners (over age 40) have stronger hearts and lungs than other women their age. *What's more,* they were in better shape, cardiovascularly, than women 20 or 30 years younger. Based on her observations, Dr. Wells concluded that physical training seems to slow the effects of aging on maximal heart rate (the highest amount of effort you can expend while exercising).

I'd like to close this chapter by emphasizing that strong, toned muscles are the key to effective living. Years ago, when I was studying advanced biology, one professor redefined "old age" by breaking the life span into four stages: infancy (ages 0 to around 20), youth (from around 20 to around 40), middle age (from around 40 to around 80) and old age (from 80 onward). One of the best ways to arrive at old age is with a well-maintained body, kept in the best shape possible with physical activity and a health-building diet.

CHAPTER 3

❖

THE AEROBIC PRESCRIPTION

The best calorie and fat burners for you

Toning your muscles is just one part of the Body Shaping equation. In an indirect but very real way, exercises that work your heart, lungs and circulatory system for more than a few minutes (collectively known as aerobics) have a bearing on your physique, too. The reason is simple: As your muscles perform continuous, rhythmic activity for prolonged periods of time (work they're *designed* to do), they use up oxygen. (*Aerobic* means "in the presence of oxygen.") At the same time, you are continuously replacing what's known as your oxygen debt—delivering a generous supply of vital O_2 molecules to your muscles.

How much oxygen you burn determines how many calories you burn.

Picture this: You decide to go for a run on your lunch hour. You start out slowly, gradually pick up the pace and find yourself going faster and faster, until your lungs can't seem to keep up with your body's demands for oxygen. You're "out of breath."

You may experience the same feeling when pedaling a bike, using a stair climber or taking an aerobics class for the first time—all activities that use the large muscles of the legs, hips, thighs and even the arms, shoulders and trunk. The more muscles involved, and the more oxygen burned, the better.

Short bursts of activity—such as a 100-meter sprint, for example, or lifting weights—tax your muscles briefly and burn up so much energy so quickly that you cannot maintain the effort for more than ten seconds or so. Instead, these efforts draw on adenosine triphosphate—sort of a chemical battery in each cell. Thus, strength training and sprinting are considered primarily anaerobic ("without oxygen"). In contrast, aerobic activity—performed not too fast or too hard but at a moderate rate—starts out anaerobically but then begins to burn up oxygen at a more economical rate.

Aerobic dance classes and step aerobics are structured, familiar types of aerobic activity. But any activity that you could conceivably perform for several hours can qualify. Bicycling, cross-country skiing, ice skating, roller skating, rowing, running, stair climbing, swimming and walking—when performed for more than a few minutes at a time—are *generally* aerobic. If you work very intensely at such activities, in a brief all-out effort, you're working anaerobically.

In fact, in real life, most efforts are neither 100 percent aerobic nor 100 percent anaerobic but a combination of both. Recent research shows that certain kinds of aerobic/anaerobic activities can provide a beneficial, aerobic effect. Activities such as tennis, racquetball and soccer—which require all-out bursts of energy followed by periods of relaxation—while not rhythmic in nature, produce similar effects.

Even weight training seems to produce some degree of aerobic effect. During recovery, after you perform your reps, your body must quickly take in more oxygen to oxidize nutrients in order to create glycogen to replenish energy used when you lift. In fact, an efficiently working aerobic system enhances recovery from weight-training sessions. So aerobics is the perfect complement to the weight-training portion of your Body Shaping program.

We'll explore the relative aerobic potential of specific activities in more detail a little further on.

THE FAT-BURNING EFFECTS OF AEROBIC EFFORT

The aerobics component of the Body Shaping program calls for a minimum of three aerobic sessions a week to start, working up to four or five sessions a week. For some, this may mean walking only a block or two to start. It won't take long for you to feel the beneficial effects. Keep up with your aerobic program—three or four times a week, at greater duration and greater intensity—and you won't run out of breath quite so quickly. And beneath the sweat, a number of important changes are occurring.

• Your lungs become more efficient at taking in oxygen and giving off carbon dioxide.

• Your blood vessels branch out, growing more capillaries to deliver oxygen-enriched blood to working muscles.

• Add strength training to aerobics, and minute powerhouses for energy known as mitochondria increase.

With these changes, you'll be able to do more repetitions of your muscle-toning exercises without getting winded. You'll be able to recover faster between exercise sets. And you'll be able to bounce back faster from your aerobic workouts, experiencing less stiffness and fatigue during your off days.

Most importantly, when you work aerobically, *you start to burn fat*. At first, your body uses up carbohydrates. Stored in the form of glycogen in the blood, muscles and liver, carbohydrates are ready for the taking and easily burned up during either the first few minutes of aerobic activity or in an anaerobic effort such as performing a weighted squat.

At any given time, however, the body's supply of carbohydrates is relatively low, and your body uses them up rather quickly. And as you become more conditioned, your body becomes more efficient; it uses available carbohydrates even more quickly and begins to attack the fat supplies. With the stepped-up release of fat from adipose tissues (body fat stores), you'll see a noticeable drop in either overall weight or at least total body fat. What's more, you will find you have more energy.

Another beneficial side effect of a regular exercise program is that when you pursue additional activities—even if it's gardening or housework—you increase what's known as your resting metabolic rate, the base level of calories your body uses up while at rest, doing nothing more than sleeping, reading and so forth. In other words, the more aerobically fit and toned you are, the more calories you'll burn when you're *not* working out.

Bear in mind, though, that the shift from a tendency toward burning just carbohydrates to burning more fat—and the accompanying boost in metabolic rate—does not occur within the first weeks of exercise. It takes a month or more. And how much your metabolic rate rises depends on how intensely you work out. If the workout is too easy, you recover quickly, and you won't significantly improve your metabolic rate. The harder you work, and the more muscle you build, the higher the metabolic rate needed to maintain muscle.

So if you want to burn calories and whittle away fat, the sooner you start some kind of aerobics program, the better.

SELECTING THE RIGHT AEROBIC ACTIVITY

So where do you start?

Aerobic dance and stepping classes seem to be the most popular forms of exercise among people who frequent the Sports Training Center and similar health clubs. Others walk, run or cycle. These seem to be convenient ways to work out, but they are by no means the only activities worth pursuing, nor are they even the best. For aerobics to work for you, you have to pick an activity that meets not one but several important criteria.

Do you enjoy it? If not, you'll drop out. Running on a treadmill is a great calorie burner, for example. But if you find it tedious and boring, you'll find all kinds of excuses to avoid it. Net calories burned: zero.

Can you work vigorously enough to work up a sweat? If you exercise vigorously, you can burn as much as 10 to 15 calories per minute! But remember, the definition of aerobic exercise is any exercise that involves "sustained, continuous, rhythmic physical activity." It's *supposed* to be hard. So intensity counts.

Along the same lines, a skilled tennis player plays vigorously enough to maintain aerobic fitness. But if you don't put a lot of power into your swing, don't hustle after every ball or stand around talking much of the time, you're not playing tennis—you're playing *at* tennis. Put more effort into the game, and learn to play well, and you'll enjoy it more *and* reap the aerobic benefits.

Is it continuous? When you walk or run, do you slow down or pause every few seconds, or do you keep up the pace for the duration? Stopping and starting is less effective than a sustained effort. (A qualifying note: Recent research suggests that intermittent stop-start efforts such as tennis or racquetball have some aerobic effect. And beginning runners may need to pause more to get their breath than trained individuals. So those activities have some value. By contrast, pitching softball doesn't produce big aerobic gains unless you pitch nonstop for a half-hour—not likely.)

Can you do it at least three times a week? Cross-country skiing is a terrific calorie burner, for example— 445 calories per hour (more if you ski fast or *up*hill). And it's a great way to add variety to your aerobics program. But do you honestly have the snow, terrain, equipment or time to do it three times a week? If not, it's not a viable option (or it's only an occasional option).

Speaking of variety, another way to avoid staleness and ensure the success of your aerobics "prescription" is to pursue different activities. For example, you might play an intense game of racquetball on Tuesday, take an aerobics class on Thursday and play tennis, run or cycle on the weekend, for example. In this way, sports can double as a wonderful, *fun* way to avoid letting your body get out of condition if you're away from your more "routine" exercises for a while.

Using more than one aerobic activity develops your cardiorespiratory endurance. Cross-training in this way has the added benefit of reducing stress on any given muscle group, thus lowering the risk of injury.

If you enjoy many sports and want to choose the best, select the activities that use the highest proportion of your total body and tax your cardiovascular system.

DOVETAILING AEROBICS WITH TONING WORKOUTS

A few minutes of running in place or another light aerobic activity is a good way to warm up for a muscle-toning workout. But ideally, you should perform full-scale, training-level aerobics the day after you weight-train. If you weight-train on Monday, Wednesday and Friday, for example, you could do aerobics on Tuesday, Thursday and Saturday. Set aside one day a week as a day of rest or only mild activity (such as a leisurely walk in the park).

If your schedule is too tight for that split routine, you can do aerobics on the same day as weight training. *In that case, do the weight training first.* That way, you'll be fresh and have the energy you need to do the toning resistance exercises properly and to tax the muscles to the safe maximum. If you do the aerobics first, you start the resistance-training workouts in a state of fatigue and don't get a quality workout.

If you do aerobics immediately after strength training, it's best to choose a noncompetitive activity such as stationary cycling, rowing, stepping, brisk walking or running. In a gym, this is easy—just move from the weight machines to the stair climber, cross-country ski machine and so forth. If your aerobic activity for the day is a competitive sport such as tennis or racquetball, do the weight training in the morning and play your game of choice in the afternoon or evening, giving your body time to recover. To play your best and avoid injury, more active sports such as racquetball are best played when you're fresh.

AVOIDING THE YO-YO EXERCISE SYNDROME

I want to emphasize that whatever aerobic activity you choose, you must learn to do it correctly and safely. Begin your workout at a low intensity and maintain that level for five to ten minutes, building up to your desired level only after your arms and legs begin to feel warm. Some other good advice:

Start out very slowly. If you've never worked out before, you can experience the aerobic effect of exercise in as little as 5 minutes. As you get into shape, it takes 20 or 30 minutes. (This is known as the training effect.) So there's no need to go all out your first day. As with strength training, you must allow your muscles to get accustomed to aerobic activity. In the first week, for example, take a short walk for about 5 or 10 minutes at a leisurely pace. Trying to go much faster would only leave your muscles too sore to work out for the rest of the week, putting the kibosh on your good intentions.

Step up the pace. The beauty of exercise is that the more you work out, the more energy you have—and the easier it becomes. The more demand you place on your muscles, the higher the demand for oxygen. The body responds by pumping more oxygen-rich blood to the tissues and removing oxygen-poor blood to the lungs to get rid of the carbon dioxide and other waste products. This is part of a process known as adaptation.

If you're a beginner, you may see positive changes in the first few months. If you are just starting to walk or run, you'll probably be out of breath after several blocks. If you persevere, however, you'll gradually build up to where you can cover several miles without discomfort.

As with the strength-training part of the Body Shaping program, the key to working aerobically is to step up your efforts and stay one step ahead of the adaptations made by your body. In order to continue to benefit from aerobics, you must progressively increase the intensity or duration of your workouts.

Increase gradually. Let your body tell you how hard to work, how far and how fast to go. If your workout leaves you overtired, you know you did too much. Back off and do only the same amount (or a little less) next time. Continue to increase the distance you can walk, the time you can ride or use the stair climber and so forth until your body gets used to the range of motion and muscles used in each activity.

Eventually, you'll build up to 30 minutes, the benchmark of an effective workout. If you get tired or feel any muscle pain, don't push on just because you haven't reached 30 minutes at a particular heart rate. Stop when your body tells you to!

On the other hand, if you can go longer and have the time for it, keep going. I started a number of people who attend my club on a walking program through the scenic hills nearby. The walk is so pleasant that they often continue to walk for up to an hour.

Cool down. If you're new to aerobics and starting out by walking a block or two only, then you don't need to cool down. But as you progress, you'll soon be working vigorously enough to elevate your heart rate and blood pressure. If you stop abruptly, blood will pool in your limbs and strain the heart. So take a lead from Olympic competitors who take an extra jog around the track after a race: Spend a few minutes jogging in place or stretching lightly to let your body gradually return to normal.

For light workouts, cooling down for a minute or so would probably suffice. But if you're working at your maximum, no less than five minutes will do.

Give yourself a break. Doing aerobics every other day leaves you time for your weight-training exercises and gives your body time off to relieve the stresses that accumulate in a single aerobic workout and over the week. (Exercising aerobically every day of the week is no more beneficial than exercising only five. And for beginners, three to five workouts is plenty.)

And don't expect to lose 5 pounds in one workout—or in one week. Your aerobic fitness develops in a wavelike manner, but over time, it will feel like a constant, straight-line improvement.

WHERE THE OXYGEN IS: AEROBICS FROM A TO Z

What follows is a series of capsule reports on 24 sports, exercises, activities and even household chores that can give you the aerobic fitness that's going to help you achieve your Body Shaping goals. The purpose here is not to dictate which activities are best (that will depend on what you like to do and how vigorously you do it). Rather, it will give you a pretty good idea of your options, relative to each other.

Caloric ranges are averages based on 30 minutes of activity performed by a 120-pound woman. The actual

ARE YOU WORKING HARD ENOUGH?

Taking a pulse and calculating target heart rate is a time-honored way of measuring exercise intensity. The simple formula: Exercisers subtract their age from 220 (the maximum heart rate). To get your minimum recommended heart rate, multiply that by 60 percent. To get your maximum, multiply by 80 percent. Then take your pulse every few minutes to see if you're working at the right level.

But if you're brand-new to aerobic exercise, don't bother measuring your heart rate for the first month or so. Instead, listen to your body. Rate your level of perceived exertion on a scale of 1 to 10 (1 being the easiest, 10 being an all-out effort).

Commonly referred to as the rate of perceived exertion, this scale was devised by Gunnar A. V. Borg some years ago. But it measured pulse rates during cardiovascular effort only. Efforts during endurance and strength training are somewhat higher. The scale represented here gives two recommended intensity zones—one for aerobic efforts and one for strength workouts.

Studies show that the rate of perceived exertion correlates well with target heart rate, without having to stop to take your pulse or do math. Instead, you will have to pay attention to how you feel as you work out. If a certain intensity feels too difficult, back off, regardless of what you "should" be doing. And don't worry if some days you don't seem to be able to work quite as hard as the previous day. In time, you'll be able to work harder and longer.

EXERCISE INTENSITY SCALE

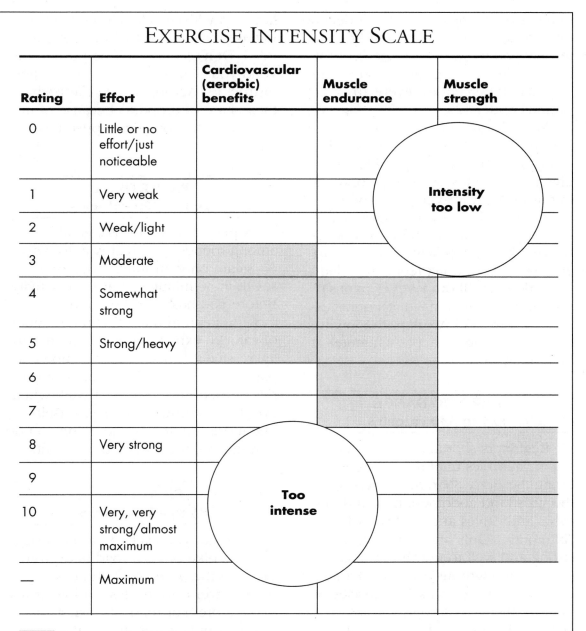

Rating	Effort	Cardiovascular (aerobic) benefits	Muscle endurance	Muscle strength
0	Little or no effort/just noticeable			
1	Very weak			
2	Weak/light			
3	Moderate			
4	Somewhat strong			
5	Strong/heavy			
6				
7				
8	Very strong			
9				
10	Very, very strong/almost maximum			
—	Maximum			

Intensity too low

Too intense

Recommended level

SOURCE: Adapted from *Medicine and Science in Sports and Exercise,* vol. 15, no. 6, 1983, and modified by M. C. Siff of the Human Performance Institute, University of Witswatersrand, South Africa, 1989.

number of calories burned will depend on your age, fitness level and how intensely you work. Add 10 percent for each additional 10 pounds you weigh; subtract 10 percent for every 10 pounds under 120.

You'll burn more calories the more vigorously you work. As with the three levels of recommended workloads given for the muscle-toning workouts in this book, however, under no circumstances should you start an aerobic activity at the highest level of intensity. Start out slowly, and work up gradually. Also, don't feel compelled to work at an all-out level of intensity for the entire session—that's unnecessary and stressful. Work in the low to moderate range with a few minutes at high intensity.

AEROBIC DANCE
125 to 330 calories

Beginners should stick to low-impact aerobics until they've been doing the Body Shaping exercises for the waist and abdomen, hips and buttocks and calves and ankles for five or six months. Only after your legs are strong and well toned should you consider more vigorous, high-impact aerobics. If you have weak leg muscles or joint problems, I strongly advise against high-impact aerobics of any kind, especially if it involves jumping on and off an exercise step.

Safety tip: Work at a pace that's right for you. Don't feel compelled to

keep up with the class if the tempo is intense for you. Rest if you feel the need. Don't let yourself be pushed beyond your limits by overly demanding instructors. Aerobic dance classes have their share of dropouts because of instructors who sometimes push too hard.

BASKETBALL
190 to 300 calories

A pickup game of basketball among friends is a great way to blow off steam on your lunch hour *and* sneak in 30 minutes of aerobic activity. Before you head for the hoops, though, keep in mind that the number of calories expended depends on how aggressively you and your competitors play. To maximize the number of calories burned, run instead of walk whenever the opportunity presents itself. The more running and jumping you do during play, the greater the benefit.

BICYCLING
85 to 450 calories

Whether you cycle on a stationary exercise bike or on a road bike, you can vary the pace. Slow and easy burns fewer calories; fast and vigorous burns more. For road enthusiasts: Cycling uphill burns more calories than riding on the flat.

If you enjoy cycling, you'll be happy to learn that the resistance-training workouts that shape your body *also* enhance your riding. If you ride a mountain bike, you should work the arms and shoulders to better support yourself and power the bike. If you prefer a road bike, which dictates a more horizontal riding position, back-strengthening exercises can help prevent aches and strains and enable you to ride longer without discomfort.

Safety tip: To avoid hip, back or knee problems, be sure to adjust the seat so that your leg is almost straight but not fully extended in the 6 o'clock position. Your knee should be slightly bent. If you fully extend the foot, your pelvis rotates to the side, straining the lower back.

CROSS-COUNTRY SKIING
215 to 900 calories

Few activities burn fat and calories like cross-country skiing, done vigorously on snow, using the whole body for a considerable period of time. Uphill sections of trails burn the max. But unless you live in snow country, you'll probably be doing most of your cross-country skiing on a ski simulator.

NordicTrack-type machines mimic the back-to-front sliding and poling motions of cross-country skiing. You still get a good workout. Don't expect to hop on a ski machine and take off like the wind, though. As with snow skiing, you may feel awkward at first: Start out slowly, then gradually increase the intensity as you gain confidence.

DANCING
85 to 300 calories

Anyone who's seen the film *Strictly Ballroom* knows that when the steps come fast and furious, ballroom dancing can work up quite a sweat. Polkas and square dancing, when pursued enthusiastically, are in the same league. The more skilled a dancer you are, the better the workout.

If you like to dance and want to work it into your aerobic program, Heel Raises, Squats and various exercises for the legs, hips and lower back can maximize the benefits.

DOWNHILL SKIING
140 to 230 calories

Cross-country skiing is customarily touted as superior to downhill skiing in terms of calories burned. But some researchers indicate that since downhill skiers tend to spend more hours on the slopes in the course of a day, they end up expending as many calories as cross-country skiers.

Needless to say, powering your way through a mogul field or blasting your way over packed powder burns more calories than cruising down the green trails. But that doesn't mean you should head for the black diamond slopes and ski beyond your ability just for the sake of burning more calories. Skiing is a great way to work an aerobic workout or two into your weekly program. But it's critical that you prepare for its rigors. I strongly recommend that preseason, you do most of the Body Shaping exercises for the legs, waist and abdomen, shoulders and back and arms, not only to prevent injury but to ski better.

To further prevent soreness in your back, calves and thighs after a day of skiing, take time to warm up, and include some stretching and active exercises before you head for the slopes.

Safety tips: To reduce the risk of injury, never ski trails beyond your ability to show off or keep up with more advanced skiers. And be aware that a slope that was well groomed in the morning can turn icy with slope traffic or changing weather, so pay attention to changing conditions throughout the day. Never come to a stop where you can't be seen by other skiers coming around a bend or over a hill in the trail. Last, if you feel fatigued, head for the lodge. The risk of a ski injury rises if you try to squeeze in one last run at the end of a strenuous day.

GARDENING AND HOUSEWORK
125 calories

Don't worry if you can't get to the gym because you have to weed the garden, dig up your irises or push your mower around the yard. These activities count! So do washing windows and mopping floors. Household chores work best as a supplement to, not a substitute for, regular workouts.

GOLF
130 to 150 calories

If you pull or carry your clubs, golf can give you a good aerobic workout. If you ride a cart, forget it. Play 18 holes, and you can burn up to 600 calories, especially if the course has hills. (Back Raises, Reverse Trunk Twists and Lat Pull-Downs can put more oomph in your stroke and help you hit the ball farther.)

HANDBALL
220 to 330 calories

Singles handball is one of the most rigorous games you can play; team handball is only slightly less of an effort. If you happen to have regular access to courts and a group of friends who like to play, handball could certainly help break the monotony of aerobics classes or other organized aerobic activities.

Safety tip: As with any game that involves a flying object traveling at top speed, wear safety goggles.

INTERVAL TRAINING
number of calories
highly variable

After a month or two of regular aerobic workouts, you may want to challenge yourself with interval training—repeated bouts of running, cycling, rope jumping or another fairly intense activity interspersed with less intense activity. Competitors use interval training to build aerobic *and* anaerobic endurance. A miler, for example, might run very fast for 440 yards, walk a lap, then repeat this cycle anywhere from five to ten times or more.

There's no reason interval training can't be part of a Body Shaping effort. Just remember to start out gradually, warm up first and increase intensity gradually, over time. The number of calories you burn will depend on intensity, number of repetitions performed and length of rest intervals. But the shorter the rest intervals, the more calories you will burn. Begin with a one-minute rest period between bursts of activity. As you get into shape, cut this to 45 seconds, then eventually 30, then 20. Also, limit interval training to one or two sessions a week.

RACQUET SPORTS
140 to 300 calories

If you like badminton, paddleball, squash or tennis, you're in luck: You can have fun while you burn calories. Don't stand around waiting for the ball or birdie to come to you, though. To get the most benefit, play hard and go after every shot.

ROPE JUMPING
220 to 235 calories

Jumping rope isn't child's play—it's quite demanding, in fact. Few people can jump rope vigorously for more than a couple of minutes without feeling burning muscle fatigue. Your best bet is to work at a moderate pace, so you don't tire out and quit.

ROWING
95 to 330 calories

The nice thing about rowing machines is that you can set your own pace—somewhere between that of tooling around a local pond trawling for bass and sculling down the Charles River. To be sure that you're involving your whole body (and thereby getting the most out of your workout), push with your legs as you pull with your arms.

Safety tips: To avoid straining your back as you row, don't bend all the way forward or backward on each stroke. Rather, keep your spine in its normal, slightly arched position, leaning forward approximately 20 degrees, then backward approximately 20 degrees. (If there's a mirror nearby, use it to check to be sure your body is in this neutral position.)

Exercises such as the Good Morning and Back Raise can strengthen the back and prepare you for rowing.

By the way, paddling a canoe or kayak offers comparable benefits. While canoeing and kayaking use the upper body only, you tend to paddle longer than you row, so total calories burned can be considerable.

RUNNING OR JOGGING
150 to 450 calories

Running burns more calories than walking and works the quads and hamstrings—great for people who want to tone their hips, thighs, calves and ankles.

Champion marathon racers average 5 minutes per mile. Other folks vary in speed from a very fast rate of 6 minutes per mile to a slow jog of 15 minutes per mile. Beginners should start at the 15 minutes per mile pace and gradually build speed as their heart, lungs and muscles get into condition.

Safety tips: Proper running form will help prevent injuries that could sideline you from your aerobic program. Stand straight and keep your arms, head and shoulders relaxed. Lean forward to accelerate only. Also, be careful not to plant the heel with the sole of your foot and your toes pointed upward. This creates a tremendous jarring effect that will eventually take its toll on your joints. Instead, land full-footed so that your heel makes contact closer to the arch and the ball of the foot, absorbing more of the impact and allowing the muscles to work more efficiently.

Also, it's best to run on forgiving surfaces such as dirt, packed gravel or asphalt track instead of concrete pavement. Buy training shoes—they have more support than racing shoes—and replace them every three months or so, before the cushioning is shot.

SLIDEBOARDING
250 to 380 calories

Technically known as lateral motion trainers, slideboards are a relatively new kind of aerobic equipment. You place special socks over your regular workout shoes and skate from side to side on a slick sheet of super-strong plastic with a bumper on each side. Athletes who cross-train to improve at more than one sport use slideboards to develop speed, strength and agility. Slideboard skating burns about the same number of calories as aerobic dance—with no impact.

While you may not care to spend a full 30 minutes on a slide, when combined with rowing, cycling, rope jumping or another aerobic activity, it's a great way to add variety to your exercise routine.

Safety tip: Don't wear ankle weights when using a slideboard—you'll build up too much momentum, overstress the hip joints and go flying.

SKATING (ICE AND IN-LINE)
150 to 300 calories

Whether you take to the ice or to the pavement, how many calories you burn skating depends on how hard you work. Since you're sliding or gliding over the surface, lack of resistance puts a cap on how much fat you can burn. But moving your arms vigorously in rhythm with your legs maximizes the workout.

SNORKELING
120 to 150 calories

Held captive on a cruise boat, chowing down the buffet fare? You can work it off by snorkeling. Few people snorkel often enough to be able to rely on it as a regular workout, though.

SOCCER, LACROSSE
AND FIELD HOCKEY
195 to 300 calories

Running, stopping, reversing direction and all the other shenanigans involved in field sports are taxing and work your heart, lungs and muscles. If you're one of the small but growing number of women who enjoy these sports, strength training can improve your playing skills.

STAIR CLIMBING/
BENCH STEPPING
165 to 350 calories

Taking the stairs instead of the elevator is standard advice to the sedentary. And before the invention of stair climber machines, weight loss experts were recommending walking up and down stairs as a simple, natural and convenient way to burn fat and calories. The average stair step is eight inches high. Stair climbing doesn't put extraordinary stress on the knees or other joints.

Safety tips: Stair climber machines

and exercise steps, however, take special considerations. On a stair climber, use a normal stepping distance, not full range, to avoid overrotating the pelvis and straining the back. Also, avoid the tendency to grab the rails—you'll burn more calories and work the legs more effectively if you stand free. If you must hold on for balance, keep it light. You want to duplicate the normal action of walking up stairs.

Similar advice goes for using an exercise step. Using an eight-inch or higher step can lead to knee or lower back problems. Do not raise your thighs higher than the horizontal. To maximize your workout, add overhead arm movements instead.

SWIMMING
135 to 400 calories

Swimming uses most of the muscles in the body, but unless you swim very fast, you won't burn a lot of calories. As with water aerobics, using hand paddles and swim fins can help you get more out of your workout. If you do add extra resistance, however, it's a good idea to do some arm- and leg-strengthening exercises to prepare your muscles for the added demand.

TREADMILL WALKING
OR RUNNING
110 to 450 calories

Don't forget treadmills as a convenient alternative to walking or running on a road, trail or track. Treadmills are a popular indoor option—*plus* you can vary the grade to increase the calorie-burning capacity of your workout. Walking at a 2 percent grade instead of the level, for example, doubles the caloric expenditure of your workout.

VOLLEYBALL
110 to 300 calories

The better you play volleyball, the more calories you can expect to burn. High-level competitors push their heart rate to the max. If you play with the intensity of two-on-two beach volleyball champs on ESPN, this is a real workout. If you're exchanging leisurely volleys with 20 of your closest friends at a Saturday afternoon picnic, you'll burn considerably less fat and fewer calories. (If you have a couple of beers after the game, it may cancel out any benefits at all.)

WALKING
110 to 250 calories

Brisk walking is one of the best aerobic choices you can make—you can do it anywhere, anytime, with no special equipment other than a good pair of made-for-walking shoes. You can burn the same number of calories as when running or jogging—you just have to walk a little longer. Walking works the hip muscles, making it the perfect complement to the Body Shaping exercises for toning the hips and buttocks. So the next time you have to go to the store, walk.

Safety tip: If you want to burn more calories while you walk, don't use ankle weights. Instead, swing your arms and take longer, faster strides.

WATER AEROBICS
110 to 310 calories

Your body weighs less in water, and the added buoyancy takes stress off joints during exercise, making water exercise a useful option for anyone who is recovering from an injury. If you've sustained a running injury, for example, you can put on a buoyancy vest and run in the deep end of the pool. The faster you run, the greater the resistance. (Your body also burns some calories trying to stay warm. And you don't have to worry about overheating.)

Moving your arms and legs through the water makes for a light and easy workout. To work a little harder and burn more calories, add push floats, pull buoys, Hydro-Tone bells, hand paddles, swim fins and other aquatic exercise devices to your routine, and move determinedly through the water. (To improvise a push float, partially fill a one-gallon plastic milk jug with water, cap it off, then push it through the water in front of you.)

❖

CHAPTER 4

TAKING INVENTORY

Setting your Body Shaping goals

The art of Body Shaping has come a long way. By combining strength training with aerobic workouts, you can firm and reshape your body as you also lose unwanted fat. It's very exciting to see these two forms of training finally coming together to produce the kind of results we're seeing today—results women were *not* able to achieve in the past through either strength training or aerobics alone.

But as effective as this new double-edged training can be, it still needs to be focused. Whether you'd like a firmer and fuller bust, a smaller waist, slimmer hips, shapelier legs (or all of the above), it's important to direct your workouts toward the specific goals you'd like to achieve. The more you can custom-tailor your workouts toward the specific changes you'd like to make, the more successful you're going to be.

The workouts in this book are organized around specific goals for specific fat spots and trouble zones. You can simply "dial in" to the exercises that are going to be most effective in helping you to achieve your particular Body Shaping objectives.

You may opt to work all your major muscle groups, thus achieving head-to-toe fitness and firmness. Many of the women I work with at the Sports Training Center do so. And invariably, they are very happy with the results: Not only do they sculpt and define areas they've chosen to improve, but also they gain overall fitness that gives them more energy, confidence and enthusiasm for everything they do.

TAKE THE BODY SHAPING INVENTORY

I suggest my clients perform a test that I've found can be as accurate as any in determining where your Body Shaping efforts might best be aimed. The head-to-toe inventory on page 38 is more accurate than stepping on a scale or even taking a body composition test. I explain why shortly.

Basically, fat takes up more space than muscle, so two people can weight 125 pounds, yet one can look trimmer and better proportioned if her body is comprised of a little more muscle and a little less fat. And of course, the whole idea behind Body Shaping is to carry your weight where you want it—a factor not reflected in a single number on the bathroom scale.

First, turn up the heat and pull down the shades, then strip down and take a long, hard look at yourself *au naturel* in a full-length mirror. Examine yourself from the front *and* the side. This takes some courage, I know. But sometimes that's what it takes to spur action. Use the table on page 38 to rate yourself.

After you've completed your evaluation, I'd suggest having several photos taken of yourself, clad in as little as possible, so you'll have a basis for comparison for your Body Shaping

progress. Maybe you already have a few such photos hidden in the bottom of a desk drawer. Fine. Either way, it can really be helpful once you embark on your Body Shaping journey to be able see exactly where it is you're coming from.

GETTING "WEIGHED" THE RIGHT WAY

Once you get into your Body Shaping program, you may be tempted to weigh yourself as a way of checking your progress. Again, evaluating yourself on the basis of weight alone is a mistake. You may see no drops on the scale whatsoever and could even see a slight weight *gain* as your workouts begin to trade fat for muscle. Since muscle weighs more than fat but occupies considerably less space, you may not be getting noticeably lighter even though you will be toning up.

A better way to monitor your progress is to keep track of how your clothes fit, take measurements of key areas such as your thighs, hips and waist and refer to your "before" photos. These benchmarks should improve regardless of whether or not you lose weight.

Another way to get a true picture of the progress you're making in your Body Shaping efforts is to make an appointment at your local health club, sports medicine clinic or physician's office for a body composition test. This is a painless yet effective way to mea-

AN AT-HOME BODY FAT TEST

To measure your percentage of body fat accurately, *at home,* I recommend a do-it-yourself device called Accu-Measure™. Using this at-home skin caliper enables you to conveniently measure your change in body fat over time. Tests show the Accu-Measure™, though simple, is as accurate as other methods, including hydrostatic testing.

At this writing, the Accu-Measure™ sells for $19.95, including instructions. To order, write: Accu-Measure, Inc., P.O. Box 4040-Y, Parker, CO 80134.

sure how much of you is fat as opposed to lean (muscle, internal organs and bone). Since you can't do anything about your vital organs and skeleton (nor would you want to!), measuring improvements in muscle mass is a scientific and valid way to gauge fat-to-muscle progress.

The test can be done by way of underwater weighing and a new electronic procedure. But the simplest and least costly method is the old "pinch" method done with skin calipers. Measurements are taken of the thickness of fat deposits at various sites such as the hips, thighs, waist and upper arms. The technician then determines your percentage of body fat based on these readings.

For most women, the average level of body fat is not a single, ideal number but a range of 20 to 28 percent. Some female marathon runners and gymnasts have been known to dip into the 10 to 15 percent range. But it's been my experience that most women look and feel their best in the area of 17 to 22 percent. So if you're looking for a target to shoot for, there it is. I would not recommend going below this, however, as you're likely to pass a point of diminishing return in terms of health, energy, psychological well-being and even appearance if you do.

To find out your percentage of body fat, ask your family doctor, a registered dietitian, an exercise physiologist or your local health club, hospital or YM/YWCA.

DON'T FORGET POSTURE

Why put the time and effort into sculpting a new body, only to skimp on the presentation? Good posture is essential to maximizing your new, ideal body. You rarely see posture emphasized in books or videos on bodybuilding, strengthening or toning. But how you carry yourself plays an especially important role in not only how you look but also how you feel. Slouching, for example, not only detracts from a well-developed chest and pushes the abdomen forward but, in doing so, also puts greater pressure on the spinal disks and nerves, causing back pain. Few people realize that

(continued on page 40)

THE BODY SHAPING INVENTORY

Problem	Acceptable	Needs some work	Needs major improvement
Chest			
Are your breasts firm and round or loose and sagging?			
Are your chest muscles well developed?			
Does your chest look elevated or sunken?			
Shoulders and back			
Are your shoulders level and square or sloped downward and/or rounded forward?			
Upper arms			
Are your upper arms firm and somewhat muscular?			
Are you satisfied with the size of your upper arms?			
Waist and abdomen			
Can you pinch an inch or less at your waist?			
Is there a distinct difference between your waist and your hips?			
Does your abdomen protrude?			

Problem	Acceptable	Needs some work	Needs major improvement
Can you see muscle tone in your abdomen?			
Hips and buttocks			
Are your hips wider than you'd like them to be?			
Are your buttocks firm?			
Are you satisfied with the size of your buttocks?			
Thighs			
Are your thighs firm and toned?			
Can you see muscle tone when you drop into a half-squat?			
Calves			
Are your calves well defined compared with your ankles?			
Do your calves become more prominent when you stand on your toes?			

poor posture contributes to fatigue. When you slouch as you walk, or slump in your chair, your muscles have to work harder to support your body. And the increased stress on your joints increases tension. Not exactly conducive to getting the most out of the Body Shaping workouts outlined in this program!

Surprisingly, the slouchy look seems to be fashionable, a trend that's actually been documented in a study by Shirley Sahrmann, professor of physical therapy and neurology at Washington University School of Medicine in St. Louis. And over time, incorrect posture, like improper nutrition, produces subtle but unhealthful changes.

So part of your inventory should include a self-test for good posture. Look in the mirror.

• Is your head held erect?

• Are your shoulders in line with your ears (not pitched forward or overextended back)?

• Is your chest held high, with the upper back erect?

Another easy way to test your posture is to stand with your back to a wall, with your heels positioned an inch or two away from the wall and your buttocks, shoulders and head lightly touching the wall. Place one hand behind your neck and the other behind your lower back. If you can move your hands forward and back more than an inch, you need to work

on your posture to restore the spine's normal curves. The Body Shaping exercises that work the thighs, hips, abdomen and lower back can help strengthen muscles that contribute to good posture.

THE GAME PLAN FOR CHANGE

So you've taken an honest and possibly eye-opening look at yourself and maybe not been too happy about what you've seen? Now what?

May I suggest you start by making a list of the specific changes you'd like to make based on your peer into the mirror. Whether it's thinner and firmer thighs, firmer and more prominent breasts, a trimmer and more muscular midsection, put your goals down on paper. The more specific and descriptive you can be, in fact, the better, because it'll help motivate you by giving you a visual image of what you're working for. What remains now is simply tuning in to the chapters devoted to the particular body areas that are of concern to you and getting started.

As I've mentioned, the exercise chapters are organized so that you can do this custom tailoring of your workouts very easily. You'll see, too, that specific advice is given on how many repetitions to do of each exercise and the amount of weight to use given the specific goals you're trying to achieve. You'll be doing more repetitions with lighter weights if size reduction and firming of a particular area are your goals and fewer "reps" with heavier weights if adding size via muscular growth is your intent. Either way, what you'll be achieving is an improvement in your body's all-important muscle-to-fat ratio, getting more of the former and less of the latter and improving not just your appearance but your fitness, your ability to burn calories, your general health and your energy and confidence levels as well.

As for the "aerobic" component of your regimen, I recommend at least three 20- to 30-minute sessions a week to help keep a rein on fat *plus* keep your heart, lungs and circulatory system in good shape. (You might call it internal Body Shaping.) Feel free to add an extra workout, however, if trimming body fat is high on your list of Body Shaping goals.

SEEING THE NEW YOU

Once you've decided on your goals, it can help to keep them in mind—and I mean that quite literally—as you begin to do the exercises that are going to bring about improvement. Imagine your thighs actually becoming smaller and firmer as you do your thigh exercises, for example, or envision your waist becoming thinner and more muscular as you do your abdominal work. The more you can bring your mind into play in your Body Shaping efforts, regardless of which part of your body you're working on, the more success you're likely to have.

Scientifically, using the mind to aid the body is known as visualization. Current research indicates that mental pictures may indeed help bring about physiological change. No doubt you've heard of people who've been diagnosed with cancer and who've used imagery to visualize their cancer cells dying, resulting in remission. Visualization may also help people with heart disease stop or reverse the buildup of artery-clogging plaque in their blood vessels.

So why not avail yourself of this same sort of boost? Put the cart before the horse by seeing yourself as you'd like to be and then keeping that image in mind as you're actually in the process of working out. Not only will you be motivating yourself on a psychological level, but also you'll be reinforcing many of the neuromuscular and biochemical mechanisms responsible for making that image become a reality.

WHAT TO EXPECT— AND HOW SOON

But so much for diagnosis. You're probably eager to get started, and that's good. But just one last word before you do.

If your physique has been years in the making, don't expect to see major changes overnight. It will be at least six to eight weeks before you begin to see any noticeable changes. So be patient and keep telling yourself it's all "money in the bank" in terms of achieving your long-term goals.

Also keep in mind that there is some fat on your body that you will never be able to lose and therefore shouldn't try. This is the fat that is characteristic of women, located in the areas of the hips, buttocks and breasts. Don't get so carried away with your Body Shaping efforts that you begin to view this fat as totally undesirable. As I've said, a body fat level of between 17 and 22 percent should be your bare minimum. Go any lower than that, and you risk losing more than you stand to gain, in terms of not just your general health but your energy levels, your menstrual regularity and your overall passion for life as well.

❖

CHAPTER 5

BODY SHAPING IMAGERY

See the results and succeed

Regardless of what your own particular Body Shaping goals may be, I think it's worth a word of caution here that you keep your goals realistic and not set yourself up for failure by trying to achieve a size or proportions that are highly unrealistic. Attempt to duplicate the physique of some super-lean celebrity, for example, and your workouts could wind up being little more than exercises in futility. Most of the super-svelte physiques you see in the movies and magazine ads and on television are the result not just of very lucky genes but of a lot more grueling exercise and highly restrictive dieting than many of these women care to divulge. These women struggle constantly to maintain their figures because their bodies, quite literally, are their lives (and livelihoods).

For her role in *Terminator 2,* as an example, Linda Hamilton lifted extremely heavy weights and went on a near-starvation diet for months to achieve the physique appropriate for that film, vowing upon completion of the movie never to put herself through that kind of torture again. She was back to living normally and regaining her natural figure the very day shooting was over.

Meanwhile, however, a magazine that detailed Ms. Hamilton's workout received more mail on that feature than any other, from women who wanted to duplicate her workout. I would venture to say that following

Ms. Hamilton's workout would leave more women sore and possibly injured than good-looking and happy with their bodies.

And not all celebs achieve their much-admired physiques through diet or exercise, either. It's no secret that many go so far as to have themselves "amended" surgically to look the way they do. They're resorting to everything from liposuction (fat removal) to breast implants and even reshaping of bone itself. These women are playing the figure control game by a whole different set of rules, so it's an unfair pressure to put on yourself to think these are the women with whom you need to "compete." Many of the superthin celebs get themselves so lean that they lose not just their sense of well-being, moreover, but also their menstrual cycles—a sign that "beauty" to such a degree is perhaps not quite what Nature had in mind.

Are these people *happy?* I think not. Most with whom I've spoken actually feel cheated, not blessed. Yes, they hear compliments from other women like "Oh, you're so thin. I wish I could be thin." But when these same women go out to eat together, the thin ones are hurting on the inside as they watch their companions eat basically what they want to eat, enjoying their meals. So often, the thin woman carefully monitors every morsel, counting calories so that she doesn't gain a few ounces (forgetting that it's *normal* for

one's weight to vary by a pound or two from day to day). She's hungry all the time. Her body isn't satisfied being so thin, yet she's very tough on herself to stay thin. That's no way to go through life.

Striving to this ideal of reedlike thinness can also have disastrous results. When I meet women who strive to be ultrathin, I think of Karen Carpenter, the singer who had such a wonderful voice but wasted away by striving to be thin. In fact, she died in the attempt. So when visualizing your ideal, don't "think thin." Rather, think of a well-shaped body with nicely defined muscles and adequate levels of body fat (about 17 to 22 percent).

EMANCIPATION FROM EMACIATION

Above all, before picking up as much as a single dumbbell, decide that you're going to be determined in your Body Shaping goals but also *realistic.* Don't make the classic mistake of wanting to achieve so much that you get discouraged and wind up achieving nothing (or worse, doing yourself harm).

The women being paraded before you by the media are unnaturally, and in many cases even unhealthfully, thin. If you find that hard to believe, consider this: A study by researchers from the University of Washington, published in the *International Journal of Eating Disorders,* found that *Playboy* centerfolds as well as Miss America contestants weigh 13 to 19 percent less than most women their age. Furthermore, over recent years, the bust, waist and hip measurements of Miss America contestants have dropped. These statistics set unrealistic standards and do women's self-image more harm than good.

Couple that with the recent declaration by the American Psychiatric Association that a body weight of 15 percent below average is a criterion for anorexia nervosa (that is, self-starvation disease), and you can see that to attempt to become "fashionably" thin is to walk a tightrope over some pretty dangerous waters.

The University of Washington researchers concluded that most women today have an unrealistic idea of how thin they should be and that these expectations may be a major cause of the epidemic of eating disorders we're seeing in American women today.

I, for one, hope that this obsession with thinness is reaching an end, however, as a fuller and more muscular look for women seems finally to be coming to the fore. "Emancipation from emaciation" is the way I look at this new demand many women are making to get their figures back, and the more I can contribute to the success of this new movement with this book, the happier I'll be. It's high time women have the same opportunities to develop their bodies as men. Down with scrawny and up with ample. Femininity should be measured not by thinness and a look of dependence and frailty but rather by strength, vitality, confidence and a passion for life itself—traits it's pretty hard to have when you're in a rubber sweat suit all day trying to subsist on diet sodas and lettuce.

TO THINE OWN BODY BE TRUE

Your one and only goal in your Body Shaping efforts should be to be the best *you* can be. As Shakespeare's Hamlet put it over 300 years ago, "To thine own self be true." Try to reshape yourself in the image of someone else, and you're only going to get discouraged. This isn't to say you shouldn't aim high and work hard. (You should.) But aim too high—as I've seen so many women do—and you risk completely missing your target.

What you need to keep in mind in designing your ideal workout schedule from the information that lies ahead is that great-looking bodies can come in many different shapes and sizes. Being truly attractive is a matter of being original and unique—maximizing your natural attributes, not trying to become something you're not. Get yourself fit and well toned, and I can guarantee that you'll not only look better but also feel better, have more energy and be healthier and more confident, whether you wind up casting the long, tall

MAGIC FAT-TO-MUSCLE MAKEOVERS

I could fill a whole other book with stories of women I know who have changed their lives for the better through exercise. Take Ann, for example: She grew up during the years when parents told their children to clean their plate. (The plate was very full to begin with.) In time, Ann grew to love eating. And it really showed. As a teenager, Ann weighed over 175 pounds—too much to show her natural attributes. But at this point, Ann liked herself and saw no need to change her body.

In her early twenties, when Ann was dating her husband-to-be, she knocked off 30 pounds through crash dieting. But like countless other women, she not only gained the weight back, she also gained an additional 10 pounds on top of the 30 she originally lost.

Ann had two children and soon weighed 200 pounds. But now she was totally disgusted. All she thought about was her weight. It interfered with her daily activities, and she and her husband began to have marital problems. Her husband left her, and she was depressed.

This time, Ann decided to exercise, not starve herself. In the beginning, it was rough and slow-going. But after a year, Ann had lost 50 pounds and couldn't remember feeling so good. More importantly, she kept her new body.

Linda is another Body Shaping success story. A large-framed woman of 35, with two children, Linda looked great before her marriage—well proportioned, with a body fat level of about 20 percent and somewhat muscular. Then she became increasingly inactive, and her body fat soared to 35 percent. Except for her calves, her well-sculpted curves were gone. I started Linda on a Body Shaping program of both strength training and a variety of aerobic activities. This was all new to Linda. But she persevered and was soon hooked. As she began to enjoy the weight-training workouts and aerobics, she started to see major changes in her body. Today, she continues to work out (she set up a mini-gym in her home) and loves herself more than ever!

shadow of a Cindy Crawford or not.

In my experience, the women who are happiest are those who *healthfully, sensibly and scientifically* reshape their bodies, not the ones who starve themselves down to skeletons. The most successful Body Shaping "graduates" are *not* thin. But they are no longer overweight or fat, and they're *very* happy.

(If you're like many women, in fact, you might not even need as much work as you think. Recent surveys show that while approximately 90 percent of women today think they're overweight, only about 25 percent actually are.)

THINKING OF YOUR NEW BODY

To increase their performance, many athletes use pre-event visualization—mental rehearsal, in other words.

A high jumper may sit in an easy chair, for example, close her eyes and visualize herself sailing over the bar higher than she has ever reached. Every detail is clear: She visualizes herself approaching the bar, taking off, flying through the air almost weightlessly, clearing the bar and landing. In the process, the high jumper is actually programming her nerves and muscles—indeed, her mind and body—to succeed. When she goes out to attempt the real thing, the effort is easier and more effective.

In the previous chapter, I explained how to use visualization to work toward individual Body Shaping goals. This technique can also help you achieve your ideal overall look. As you launch your Body Shaping program, see yourself as you want to look in the future. See yourself walking and talking with this new body, at work and at play—more muscle here, less fat there. Picture yourself dressed up the way you would like to look in a particular dress or outfit, socializing with friends. In essence, if you see yourself as the best in whatever you do, including Body Shaping, you, too, can be a champion.

CHAPTER 6

WEIGHTS, REPS AND SETS

A three-step plan for toning and shaping

U ntil now, we've focused on the "what" and "why" of Body Shaping; now we'll explain the "how." In the seven chapters that follow, I'll be giving you exercises that represent "the state of the art in sweating smart" for virtually every major muscle of your body—not routines lifted from some movie star's day planner but rather a scientific workout formula based on years of research into the very best ways to shape and tone muscles.

I'm not knocking all celebrity-based programs. But their dismal success rate suggests that something is fundamentally wrong somewhere. Surveys show that we're in worse shape as a nation today than we were before all these photogenic fitness buffs started espousing their message of "no pain, no gain" over 20 years ago. We've "gained," all right, but not in the way anticipated. The average American adult has put on approximately *6 pounds of fat* since all the grunting and groaning first began. In fact, you might say that the alleged fitness "boom" has been more of a fitness "bust," thanks in large part to this "path of pain" exercisers were once implored to follow.

SLOW AND EASY DOES IT

Am I suggesting that achieving a trimmer and firmer body is a stroll down easy street?

No. But I am saying that it doesn't

have to be (and, in fact, should not be) torture, either. For one thing, the principle "no pain, no gain" goes against human nature: Instinct tells us to avoid pain ("Don't touch that hot stove!"). And it goes against human physiology: Pain is a sign that on a cellular level, tissues are being damaged. In the case of exercise, pain means that muscles (and usually the tendons that serve those muscles) are undergoing damage—hardly the goal of a fitness effort.

Add the psychological obstacles associated with a fitness program that's rooted in pain, and it's not hard to understand why the "no pain, no gain" philosophy has failed to "whip" so many people into shape. It's been my experience—and research supports me on this—that exercisers who consistently attempt to "go for the burn" will, in fact, "burn out" far short of reaching their fitness goals. The pain of their workouts "rewards" them with only more pain later in the form of soreness or injury, so no wonder they toss in the towel.

Is that any way to get a body fit?

You bet it's not. The fitness "kick" that can work is the one that doesn't do any "kicking" at all. Rather, the most effective program is one that gently coaxes the body, giving it ample time to make the intricate biochemical changes that optimal muscular toning and development require.

As I frequently need to remind

some of the more gung-ho women at the Sports Training Center, shaping and toning the body is a process that goes more than just skin-deep. In fact, the visible changes you see are just the tip of the iceberg compared with all the complex internal changes that you cannot see—blood vessels branching out into greater numbers of capillaries to give better service to your newly active muscles, for example, or ligaments and tendons increasing in thickness and strength to protect joints from injury. As you work out regularly, even the way you metabolize food will change in order to improve the availability of glycogen (blood sugar) as fuel for your workouts.

All of which takes time. There simply is no way of hurrying these important changes, no matter how much "pain" you're willing to endure. Try to rush these adaptations, in fact, and you risk slowing them down, as your body will respond with injury or soreness as a way of protecting itself against what it rightly perceives as abuse. The body can be coaxed, you see, but it will rebel if coerced.

GETTING STARTED

As we discussed in chapter 2, high reps with light weights is the secret to muscular leanness, while fewer repetitions with heavier weights creates muscular size. So keep these general rules in mind as you tailor your ideal Body Shaping workout.

• If you want an area smaller and tighter—abdomen, waist or hips, for example—do all the abdominal, waist or hip exercises each time you work out.

• If you want to build up an area—such as your chest, for example, or your calves, to give your legs more shape—do fewer repetitions using heavier weights *and* more reps with light weights.

If you've had any experience with weight training at all, you may be accustomed to reading or hearing standard advice like "Do three sets of 10 reps" for each exercise. My program isn't based on a generic standard—it's pegged toward individual goals and progress. And it's less work. A workout wedded to the standard of "three sets of 10" not only is something of a marathon physically; it's a marathon time-wise as well. To do three sets of 10 reps for the 15 or so exercises that a good total body workout requires can easily take an hour and a half—more time than a lot of women can spend, and more time than they *need* to spend.

I'm convinced the main reason weight-training programs have not been more popular with women until lately is that the regimens suggested are simply not realistic for most women's busy lifestyles. Nor are they properly designed for the figure modifications most women really want to make. Trying to look like Tarzan is one thing, but it's my guess that most of you simply would rather look like Jane.

The Level 1, Level 2 and Level 3 workouts recommended in the chapters ahead are geared with this in mind. They're not finite numbers; they're *ranges* within which you progress at your own pace, according to your own needs. After all, these are workouts that will not increase the size of your muscles so much as they will simply improve your muscles' firmness and shape. (Some women will, however, notice greater muscularity with Level 2 and Level 3 workouts.)

If you do want to build up certain areas, then do Level 3 workouts. These are somewhat more strenuous, as you'll see, but still well within reach if you work up to them. (No shortcuts allowed.)

Make no mistake about it, though—Levels 1 and 2 are *not* wimpy efforts. They require plenty of energy and will achieve the Body Shaping goals of most women—firmer, sleeker, more shapely and better defined. These workouts will help whittle away fat as they tighten and give better shape to the muscles hidden by that fat. Let's take a closer look now at the levels and the work they'll require.

LEVEL 1: LAYING THE FOUNDATION

If you've never trained with weights, start at this level, even if you're already aerobically fit thanks to other activities such as jogging, walking, swimming or aerobics class. If

REMEMBER TO BREATHE!

When you begin your Body Shaping workouts (at Level 1, with light weights), how you breathe isn't terribly critical. As you increase the amount of weight you lift, however, how you breathe is more important. So you should develop proper breathing patterns from the start.

The instructions for the Body Shaping workouts tell you to inhale on the exertion (the hardest part of the exercise, working against gravity), hold briefly and exhale on the return, staying in control of the weight. But don't be surprised if you read or hear the opposite from other sources—that you should exhale on exertion and inhale on return.

The widely recommended practice of exhaling on exertion is based on theory, not research. It's true that if you hold your breath with your glottis (that is, the opening between the vocal cords) closed for too long (up to eight seconds), you could pass out. That's because the internal pressure in the chest and abdomen increases when you hold your breath on exertion, and if it increases greatly, it squeezes down on the blood vessels shuttling blood and oxygen to and from the heart. This can and does happen, and people can black out. But if you breathe correctly (without holding your breath for more than one or two seconds, tops), inhaling on exertion is not dangerous.

There has never been a study on weight lifters in the United States showing that it's better to inhale on the return. On the contrary: A roundtable discussion by experts from the National Strength and Conditioning Association unanimously agreed that breath holding is part of the weight-lifting effort. Inhaling and holding the breath briefly on exertion—any exertion, for all sports—comes naturally: In his book *The Athlete's Breathing*, V. V. Mikhilov found that whenever athletic skills were executed properly, athletes held their breath. Not for long, of course—we're talking about a second or two, no more.

Inhaling on the exertion:
- Provides greater force (up to 20 percent, according to several studies).
- Stabilizes the spine and helps prevent lower back injuries.
- Transforms the trunk (and, in fact, the whole body) into a stable base against which your arms and legs can move properly.

So the breathing instructions provided help you in three ways. Follow them carefully, especially if you move up to the heavier weights.

you've been working out to some degree, you probably won't stay at this level for very long. But you should definitely start with Level 1 in order to avoid muscle soreness or injury. Weight training puts stress on muscles, ligaments and tendons that's not encountered in many other fitness activities. So even though you may be an aerobic dynamo, swallow your pride for the time being and have the sense to begin your weight-training efforts at this first level.

And remember, "gain without pain" is the rule of thumb. You'll be working at a level that will be preparing your body for the more visible changes to come. What this will mean specifically is starting with just 2, 3 or 4 repetitions of each exercise for the first workout, and *that's all*. Even if you feel capable of doing more, resist the urge to work harder for now, because you're likely to pay for it in soreness.

After your first three or four sessions, you may add 1 or 2 more repetitions per workout. But proceed carefully. In these early stages, the idea is to proceed slowly and methodically, to give your body time to adapt to the new demands placed on your muscles. *If you experience any sort of discomfort at all the day after a workout, take it as a sign that you've attempted to progress too fast.*

The exercises described typically suggest a certain amount of weight (or a range) with which to begin—2- to 5-pound dumbbells, for instance. Do not increase the amount of weight you use for any given exercise until you've progressed from Level 1 to Level 2. Assume you're working out three times a week, for example, and you've increased your number of repetitions by one for each exercise after the first week. This means you shouldn't even be thinking about weight increases for at least the first month. I know this can seem like slow-going, but trust me: You have more to lose than gain by rushing things. You can build all that much stronger a house by taking the time to lay a good, solid foundation.

LEVEL 2: TRIMMING AND TONING

Reaching Level 2—15 to 20 repetitions—takes longer for some exercises than others. When you reach this point, you can gradually increase your weights.

While considerable amounts of firming, toning and shaping occur at Level 2, you don't necessarily need to proceed to Level 3 in order to substantially firm and tone your muscles. You can still firm up, trim down and get stronger doing "just" 15 to 20 reps with relatively light weights. In fact, I know many women who prefer to stay at Level 2 and are satisfied with the results they get.

Should 15 to 20 reps at Level 2 become too easy and you want to advance to Level 3, simply add 2 to 5 pounds per exercise. This will make the 15 to 20 repetitions you've been doing considerably more difficult. In fact, don't be surprised if you find yourself doing fewer reps. That's okay—it's all part of the plan. You'll grow stronger as you once again build up to 15 to 20 repetitions.

Once you are able to do 20 reps with added weight, you may want to stay there—or you can bump up the weight again by another 2 to 5 pounds, hence coaxing even more endurance and strength from your body over and above what you can expect to achieve at Level 1.

Racheting up the weights-and-reps ladder like this is, appropriately enough, known as progressive weight training—the amount of weight you're able to lift gradually increases. And at this point, you'll begin to see measurable improvement in firmness, endurance, strength and energy.

While many women see substantial changes in musculature after working out at Level 2 for two or three months, you may not experience any noticeable increases in muscular size. For more muscle mass, you'll need to move up to Level 3.

LEVEL 3: GOING FOR ADDITIONAL SCULPTING

For many women, looking firm but still feminine is the extent of their weight-training goals. So if Level 2 meets your needs, fine. But I suggest you keep one thing in mind. For certain trouble spots, you can customtailor your physique by enlarging some areas while reducing others, thereby sculpting your body in ways not possible at lower levels.

If you'd like a larger and fuller bosom, for example, you can achieve it by progressing to Level 3 for exercises that specifically work the chest area. Or if you'd like to give your legs more shape or help compensate for thick ankles, you can build them up by working the quads of the front of the thighs at Level 3.

In this way, muscular growth can be achieved preferentially and strategically, not only preserving but also *accentuating* a feminine shape. This is what I recommend for many women once they've reached and mastered Level 2 (and I've seen it produce some remarkable results).

RECOMMENDED WORKLOADS: GUIDE, NOT GOSPEL

The instructions for each workout recommend specific amounts of weight to use, the number of sets to do plus the number of repetitions to perform within these sets. Please keep in mind, however, that these are recommendations only. Feel free to adjust them slightly up or down to suit your particular capabilities. Be respectful of—but not ruled by—the numbers.

At Level 3, the workloads increase considerably. So you should always begin with a warm-up set to adequately prepare your muscles for the work at hand. As a general rule, use approximately half the weight used in the second set, the strength set, to warm up. Example: If you do 8 reps with 20 pounds in the second set, you would use half that amount—10 pounds—in the first set, your warm-up set.

At Level 3, it's also important to do the strength work (set 2—fewer reps, higher weights) before the toning work (set 3—more reps, less weight). If you were to do the toning reps before the strength reps, your muscles would be too fatigued for you to perform the kind of quality set that's conducive to muscle growth.

A Sample Head-to-Toe Body Shaping Workout

What might a good, whole body workout look like—one that gets to virtually every major muscle group?

Here's one that I often recommend at the Sports Training Center. You needn't follow it to the letter. But if your goal is complete body conditioning, the more closely you follow it, the better. Combined with two or three 30-minute aerobic workouts a week (see chapter 3), this workout would leave no muscle "unturned."

Problem area	Recommended workout
Shoulder "caps" (deltoids)	Lateral Arm Raises (page 87)
Front of the upper arms (biceps)	Biceps Curls (page 101)
Back of the upper arms (triceps)	Triceps Push-Downs (page 105)
Back of the shoulders and upper triceps	Triceps Kickbacks (page 105)
Forearms and wrists	Wrist Curls and Reverse Wrist Curls (page 105)
Sides of the upper and lower back ("lats")	Lat Pull-Downs (page 87)
Middle of the upper back	Reverse Flies (page 87)
Chest muscles (pectorals)	Bench Presses (page 67)
Lower back	Back Raises (page 121)
Sides of the waist (abdominal obliques)	Reverse Trunk Twists (page 121)
Upper abdominals	Curl-Ups (page 115) and Modified Curl-Ups (page 118)
Lower abdominals	Reverse Sit-Ups (page 118)
Buttocks and back of the upper thighs	Hip Extensions (page 135)
Sides of the hips	Leg Abductions (page 155)
Back of the thighs	Leg Curls (page 152)
Front of the thighs	Leg Extensions (page 148)
Back of the lower legs (calves)	Seated Calf Raises (page 186)

Note: At Levels 1 and 2, there's less stress on the muscles. So you don't need to do a warm-up set. But you still need to do some kind of light aerobic work to warm up overall. (See page 56 for details.)

How much weight you actually use for any given exercise will depend on how strong you are. And the exact number of repetitions will depend on the exercise, your fitness level and how well you've mastered the technique for that exercise.

What's more important than the numbers is how the exercises make you feel when you're doing them. You should experience some strain in completing these recommended sets, but not massive struggle. If any of the workout loads I recommend does seem too difficult, or if it leaves you feeling stiff or sore the next day, the workload has been too great and should be reduced. Use a slightly lighter weight for the exercise next time, or simply do fewer repetitions of it.

To sum up: Three levels of training are given for each of the exercises presented for various trouble zones—chest, shoulders and back, arms, waist and abdomen, hips and buttocks, thighs and calves and ankles. Use this guide when progressing toward your goals.

Level 1: Three to 4 repetitions of each exercise, adding 1 or 2 reps per workout until a capability of 15 to 20 reps is reached.

Purpose: To achieve a basic, entry-level muscle-toning program and lay the necessary physiological foundation for progressing to Levels 2 and 3.

Level 2: Fifteen to 20 repetitions of each exercise, increasing the weight used by approximately 2 to 5 pounds each time 15 to 20 reps becomes relatively easy.

Purpose: To tone muscle further and enhance strength beyond what could be attained at Level 1.

Level 3: Three sets of each exercise, starting with a warm-up set. In set 2, use heavier weights for comparatively fewer repetitions, and in set 3, use less weight for more repetitions.

Purpose: To develop added muscle and toning in specific areas where size is desirable.

ADDING HERE, SUBTRACTING THERE: THE BODY SHAPING PRESCRIPTION

Many women who consult me do Level 3 (muscle-building) workouts for areas they want larger (say, the bust) and Level 2 trimming and toning work for areas they want smaller (such as the hips, buttocks or waist). Over time, it's amazing what this "addition/subtraction" technique can achieve.

If you decide this is the Body Shaping tactic you'd like to take, the basic formula to keep in mind is very simple: More repetitions with lighter weights for achieving leanness, and fewer repetitions with heavier weights for achieving growth. You can literally be your body's own "sculptor"—within your genetic limitations regarding number and kind of muscle fibers, of course.

Take the case of Jennifer as an example.

Jennifer was moderately overweight, with relatively small breasts but fairly large buttocks and hips. She wanted to know if there was any way to improve her pear-shaped proportions. So I suggested the following Body Shaping program.

- 20 minutes of calorie-burning aerobic work such as walking three to five times a week (to help reduce her amount of body fat overall)
- Level 2 weight training using the Hip Abduction, the Leg Extension and other exercises to tighten and trim her buttocks and hips
- Level 3 weight training using the Incline Press, the Bench Press and other exercises for the chest

Jennifer progressed to this workout schedule gradually, spending a month at Level 1 and another two to three months at Level 2. At that point, she began to see some very favorable results and considered the time spent well worth it. One year after starting the program, Jennifer happily commented that she "now casts a significantly more shapely shadow."

To keep track of your own Body Shaping regimen, use the exercise log at the end of this chapter. Every time you work out, record the amount of weight and number of reps and sets you do for each exercise. (If you need more space, feel free to make extra copies.)

WARM UP TO WORK OUT

A relaxed muscle is a healthy muscle. If your workouts leave your muscles overly tense and tight for hours, something is wrong. Also, it's very stressful for the body to go abruptly from a state of rest to highly vigorous activity. As with aerobics, it's important to prepare the muscles for work before doing your Body Shaping weight workouts.

A few minutes of walking or jogging in place while circling your arms increases blood circulation to the muscles and stretches the muscles so that they can lengthen and contract more easily, reducing muscle soreness, preventing injury and enhancing postworkout recovery.

Other effective ways to warm up include:

- Doing jumping jacks.
- Peddling a stationary bike lightly.
- An easy walk on a treadmill.

If you're starting at Level 1, you'll need to warm up for just five minutes or so. At this level, working out with little or no weight in itself serves as a warm-up. If you move up to heavier weights—to Level 2 or 3—you should tailor your warm-up accordingly. Listen to your body, and warm up as much as you feel is necessary to prepare your muscles for the effort.

You may want to include active stretches in your warm-up routine, especially as you advance. Stretching prepares the muscles for work, increasing your flexibility and enabling you to perform the exercises correctly, through a greater range of motion.

Doing one or two half-squats before performing the Body Shaping exercises for the thighs, hips, buttocks or calves, for example, stretches the muscles needed for those exercises. Similarly, doing Biceps Curls or Triceps Kickbacks with very light (1- to 2-pound) weights can gently stretch your muscles before you tackle the hefty stuff.

A caution about pre-exercise stretching: Never stretch a "cold" muscle. Stretch *after* you warm up (especially if your muscles are very tight) and before you start your actual weight-lifting routine. Hold for 30 seconds, then relax. Don't bounce. Otherwise, you risk overstretching. (Some people stretch without warming up, but I strongly advise against it—stretching alone does not fully prepare muscles for work.)

COOL DOWN TO WIND DOWN

If you're just starting out—doing only four or five exercises per session with little or no weight—you're probably not going to work up much of a sweat or get your heart pumping too hard. If you work up to more demanding routines, however, with little rest in between exercises, your heart rate is bound to increase. That's perfectly normal—it shows you're putting some muscle into your program. But as you finish your workout sessions, it's important not to stop abruptly. If you stop cold, your blood will pool in your legs and other muscles, stressing your vascular system. Instead, help your body return to its normal resting state gradually. Walk around the gym, shaking your arms and legs, to help release tension built up during strength training. Let your pulse return to normal, and you will literally cool down.

Don't skimp on the cool-down: If you're working very hard and getting your pulse up to 180 or higher, you should allow about five minutes to bring your heart rate down to normal. If, however, you raise the heart rate only slightly, to 90 or 100, it should take just a minute or so to get back to normal.

It's not a bad idea to cool down slightly in between sets or exercises, either. Letting the muscles relax helps flush out some of the waste products that build up during effort. At the same time, a short cool-down period energizes the muscles, helping you get a higher-quality workout.

Cooling down is the opposite of warming up, but the principle is the same: Any change from one state (intense) to another (rest) should be gradual. So don't skip or rush your warm-up or cool-down.

Body Shaping Workout Log

Date EXERCISE	Wt.	Reps / Sets	Wt.	Reps / Sets	Wt.	Reps / Sets	Wt.	Reps / Sets	Wt.	Reps / Sets

BODY SHAPING WORKOUT LOG

Date

EXERCISE	Wt.	Reps/Sets	Wt.	Reps/Sets	Wt.	Reps/Sets	Wt.	Reps/Sets	Wt.	Reps/Sets	Wt.	Reps/Sets

BODY SHAPING WORKOUT LOG

Date

EXERCISE	Wt.	Reps / Sets	Wt.	Reps / Sets	Wt.	Reps / Sets	Wt.	Reps / Sets	Wt.	Reps / Sets	Wt.	Reps / Sets

BODY SHAPING WORKOUT LOG

Date

EXERCISE	Wt.	Reps / Sets	Wt.	Reps / Sets	Wt.	Reps / Sets	Wt.	Reps / Sets	Wt.	Reps / Sets	Wt.	Reps / Sets

BODY SHAPING WORKOUT LOG

Date

EXERCISE	Wt.	Reps/Sets	Wt.	Reps/Sets	Wt.	Reps/Sets	Wt.	Reps/Sets	Wt.	Reps/Sets	Wt.	Reps/Sets

❖

CHAPTER 7

THE CHEST

Gravity-defying techniques to improve your bustline

I had to appreciate Janet's sense of humor, if not necessarily her anatomical accuracy. "I see now why they call the female chest a bust," she said. "No matter what kind of breasts you start out with, things get only worse with age."

A mother of three in her late thirties, Janet was lamenting what she called the collapse of her once firm and shapely breasts. Her bust had gone from high and full to low and empty, and she was considering cosmetic surgery to restore what she felt was rightfully hers. "I want the old me back," she said. "It doesn't seem fair that I should be penalized for having put my breasts to good use."

Janet had breastfed her three children, which is what she meant by

"good use." And Janet was right—nursing changes the breasts. When the mammary glands fill them with milk, the breasts expand and put added strain on the ligaments that give them their firmness and shape. But large breasts are subject to the same strain, even in nonlactating women. Wearing a bra that provides too little support can add to the problem, as I told Janet.

In other words, nursing mothers aren't the only women who experience a gradual loss of shape. Gravity, after all, is democratic.

HOPE FOR THE LESS-THAN-VOLUPTUOUS

But I could see that Janet didn't find my words heartening. "Which means what, Dr. Yessis? That I'm destined to stay this way—and maybe even get worse—unless I take the surgical leap?" she asked.

As we talked further, it became clear that Janet was not totally comfortable with all aspects of the surgical solution. And her concerns went beyond the risks and cost (which give many people pause, as well they should). Janet had what you might call

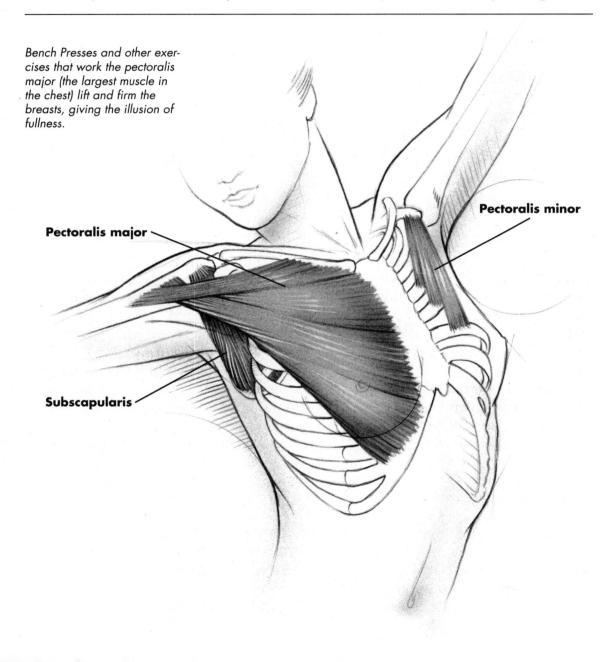

Bench Presses and other exercises that work the pectoralis major (the largest muscle in the chest) lift and firm the breasts, giving the illusion of fullness.

Pectoralis major

Pectoralis minor

Subscapularis

some "philosophical" considerations about breast improvement surgery. In her mind, there was something "ungenuine" about lifts and implants, she said. Which was why she was coming to me. Janet wanted to know the *truth* about what she might be able to accomplish through a disciplined exercise program. "I'm willing to invest the time and effort," she said, "but only if I'm going to get results."

A NONSURGICAL BREAST LIFT

I liked Janet's attitude. Here was a woman who knew what she wanted and was willing to work in order to get it. "Let's put it this way," I told her. "You can do a lot more to improve your bust with exercise than the 100,000 or so women who opt for surgical refurbishing every year may realize."

The reason is simple: The breasts are composed primarily of fat layered over muscle——the two most "negotiable" types of body tissue we have. Yes, there are some mammary glands within the breasts, but only about a teaspoon's worth, which is why breast size has little to do with the ability to nurse an infant. And yes, there are a certain number of ligaments to provide support. Mostly, however, the breasts are just fat and underlying muscle. So they're subject to the same fat-burning, muscle-building effects of exercise and weight loss as any other part of the body—hips, waist, buttocks and so forth.

"But what about stretched-out supporting ligaments?" was Janet's thoughtful reply. "You can't exercise those back into shape, can you?"

Janet was right. You can't. But you can stop (or at least minimize) further stretching of these ligaments by reducing breast fat.

And even if your problem is a flat, not sagging, chest, building the muscle beneath the breasts (known as the pectoralis) can give you a larger, fuller and more prominent bust. (For proof, just look at the overdeveloped chests on male bodybuilders, who have more of a "bust" than some women.)

At this point, Janet appeared encouraged. "What have I got to lose? I'll try your program," she said. "The surgeon will have to wait."

A year later, Janet was 20 pounds lighter—mainly through the hips and waist—yet her bosom was noticeably fuller and firmer. Janet had worked hard and was pleased with the results. *But she didn't do anything you can't do.* She simply performed the scientifically proven, *bodybuilder-tested* exercises presented in this chapter.

As you'll see, the exercises are divided into three categories—those for the upper chest, middle chest and lower chest. Because in order to achieve optimum results, the chest muscle—like many muscles of the body—consists of sections that must be developed *separately* and *collectively*. In other words, to improve results in any given muscle group, you have to do specific exercises for each muscle in that group.

As with reshaping other areas of the body, this is the little-known secret of true Body Shaping success.

INCLINE PRESS
(for the Upper Chest)

This exercise is especially effective for toning the muscles of the upper part of the chest, thus helping to give

---

INCLINE PRESS USING DUMBBELLS

Recommended Workloads

Level 1: One set of 2 to 3 repetitions, to start
Level 2: One set of 15 to 20 repetitions
Level 3: Set 1—10 repetitions with half the amount of weight used in set 2
      Set 2—8 to 10 repetitions maximum
      Set 3—15 to 20 repetitions maximum

Sit on an incline bench with your feet flat on the floor, shoulder-width apart. Hold dumbbells (or a barbell) with palms facing forward.

Inhale, then raise the weights directly upward until your arms are fully extended. Exhale as you lower the weights back down to your chest (as in previous photo). Repeat.

BENCH PRESS USING A BARBELL

Recommended Workloads

Level 1: One set of 2 to 3 repetitions, to start
Level 2: One set of 10 to 15 repetitions
Level 3: Set 1—10 repetitions with half the amount of weight used in set 2
          Set 2—8 to 10 repetitions maximum
          Set 3—15 to 20 repetitions maximum

(1)

Lie on your back on a padded weight bench (1). Your feet should be flat on the floor, shoulder-width apart, and your knees should be bent at approximately a 90-degree angle. There should also be a slight (not abnormal) arch in your lower back. Grasp the barbell as it sits in its rack over your head, using an overhand grip. Your hands should be slightly wider apart than the width of your shoulders.

(2)

Lift the barbell out of the rack, as shown (2).

(continued)

the top of the breasts a fuller, rounded look. As a bonus, the Incline Press also works the muscles of the shoulders (the anterior and middle deltoids) and portions of the back of the upper arms (triceps), giving firmness to these parts of the body as well.

To do the exercise, you can use either two dumbbells (shown on page 66) or a barbell and still achieve the same effects.

You don't have to use heavy weights for the Incline Press; performing these moves correctly is the key to optimum results. If you're just starting out, you shouldn't do this exercise with more than about 10 pounds (total, not in each hand). So if

---

BENCH PRESS USING A BARBELL — CONTINUED

Inhale slightly and lower the bar slowly, keeping it under control and allowing your elbows to point out to the sides as the bar nears your chest (3). However, do not allow the bar to touch your chest.

At this point, begin raising the bar back up, exhaling as it passes the most difficult part of its return trip, which will probably be slightly beyond the midway point (4). Continue this upward movement until your arms once again are fully extended. Relax for a second or two, then repeat.

you're using dumbbells, begin with approximately 2 to 5 pounds. Or use a barbell with no added weight. (If the only barbell you have is Olympic-size, which can weigh as much as 45 pounds, use dumbbells instead.)

If you're using dumbbells, you can add variety to the workout by lifting first one arm, then the other. The total number of reps is the same.

BENCH PRESS
(for the Mid-chest)

Bench Presses work the middle portion of the chest. The lifting instructions (see page 67) use a barbell, but they also apply if you use dumbbells or a bench press machine. (As with the Incline Press just described, if the only single barbell to which you have access is Olympic-size, use dumbbells weighing 2 to 5 pounds each instead.)

For safety, it's advisable to have a spotter present when you're using a barbell, to help you return the bar to its rack should you be unable to do so. This is especially true should you progress to using heavier weights.

Avoid the tendency to arch your back to assist in doing Bench Presses. Overarching the spine can be dangerous and detracts from the effectiveness of the exercise. Another potentially dangerous maneuver is to allow the bar to bounce off your chest to assist its return trip upward. Again, consider this not only a detriment to the effectiveness of the exercise but also

risky: You could bruise or crack a rib or your sternum (chest bone) or perhaps even bruise the breasts.

BENCH PRESS USING DUMBBELLS
(for the Mid- or Upper Chest)

As mentioned, Bench Presses can be done with dumbbells instead of a barbell (see page 70). Using dumbbells eliminates the risk of getting pinned beneath a barbell you've become too exhausted to lift. But the other advantage is that by modifying your grip, you can use this exercise to work either the mid-chest or the upper chest: Turning your hands inward works the muscles of the upper chest while turning them forward works more of the middle portion of the chest.

Begin with dumbbells weighing 2 to 5 pounds.

SEATED BUTTERFLY
(for the Mid-chest)

Another good exercise for developing the muscles of the middle portion of the chest is done on a seated butterfly machine (sometimes known as a pec deck).

The instructions on page 72 are specific to a machine called the Keiser, but other machines—such as Cybex, Maxicam and Universal—are very similar. With machines other than the Keiser, you have to set your resistance level prior to positioning yourself. If this is the case, you should have someone help you bring the machine's arm pads slightly forward, so you do not have to begin the exercise with your arms extended back too far. That puts strain on the shoulders and risks the development of stretch marks on your chest and shoulders.

PULLOVER
(for the Lower Chest)

To achieve a full-breasted "cantaloupe" look, you have to work the lowest portion of the chest muscle (pectoralis), illustrated on page 64.

BENCH PRESS USING DUMBBELLS

Recommended Workloads

Level 1: One set of 2 to 3 repetitions, to start
Level 2: One set of 10 to 15 repetitions
Level 3: Set 1—10 repetitions with half the amount of weight used in set 2
Set 2—8 to 10 repetitions maximum
Set 3—15 to 20 repetitions maximum

Lie on a padded weight bench with your feet flat on the floor about shoulder-width apart. Hold the dumbbells at chest level, using either a forward grip (left) or an inward grip (below).

One of the best exercises for doing this is the Pullover, done with a single dumbbell (see page 74). It's also one of the best exercises for expanding the rib cage underneath the chest, which is underdeveloped in many women.

CABLE PULL-DOWN (for the Lower Chest)

Performed on a high cable pulley machine, this is another good exercise for the lower chest (see page 75). As with the previously described exer-

Inhale and raise the dumbbells until your arms are fully extended. Exhale after passing the most difficult part of the lift. Pause in the top position, then inhale as you lower the weights back down to your chest. Pause for a second, then repeat.

cises, beginners should start with no more than 5 to 10 pounds of weight total—an amount that allows you to do the recommended number of repetitions for your level without a great deal of difficulty.

CABLE CROSSOVER
(for the Mid- and Lower Chest)

Performed on a double cable machine (see page 76), this is yet another good exercise for developing the

(continued on page 77)

SEATED BUTTERFLY USING A PEC DECK

Recommended Workloads

Level 1: One set of 3 to 4 repetitions, to start
Level 2: One set of 10 to 15 repetitions
Level 3: Set 1—10 repetitions with half the amount of resistance used in set 2
Set 2—8 to 10 repetitions maximum
Set 3—15 to 20 repetitions maximum

Adjust your seat height so that your arms form a 90-degree angle at the elbows and shoulders when the forearms are placed against the resistance pads. Your feet should be placed so that they're able to make contact with the controls for adjusting resistance, which should be set at zero to start. (On machines other than a Keiser, your feet should be flat on the floor.)

To begin, bring the resistance pads forward.
Then adjust the resistance to the level you desire.

Inhale slightly and slowly move your arms back until
they're in line with your shoulders. Don't let your
arms extend so far back that you feel an uncomfortable stretching across your chest. Instead, stop
when your arms are in line with your shoulders, not
beyond, and then push forward.

PULLOVER USING A SINGLE DUMBBELL

Recommended Workloads

Level 1: One set of 2 to 4 repetitions, to start
Level 2: One set of 10 to 15 repetitions
Level 3: Set 1—10 repetitions with half the amount of weight used in set 2
   Set 2—8 to 10 repetitions maximum
   Set 3—15 repetitions maximum

Lie on a padded weight bench with your feet flat on the floor, shoulder-width apart. Grasp one end of a dumbbell with both hands and raise it directly overhead, with arms fully extended. This is the starting position.

Inhale deeply as you lower your arms backward until the dumbbell reaches a point level with or slightly below the level of your back. Allow your arms to bend just enough to prevent painful stress on your elbows. As you lower the weight, inhale deeply to expand your rib cage. Then return the dumbbell to overhead and exhale. Relax and repeat.

PULL-DOWN USING A HIGH CABLE PULLEY MACHINE

Recommended Workloads

Level 1: One set of 2 to 3 repetitions, to start
Level 2: One set of 10 to 15 repetitions
Level 3: Set 1—10 repetitions with half the amount of resistance used in set 2
Set 2—8 to 10 repetitions maximum
Set 3—15 to 20 repetitions maximum

Stand an arm's length away from the front of the machine. Hold the bar with your hands approximately shoulder-width apart (or less) in a narrow over-hand grip. Inhale as you pull the bar down with your elbows slightly bent.

Pull the bar down about as far as your thighs, then exhale as you allow the bar to return to its starting position. Pause, then repeat.

Crossover Using a Double Cable Machine

Recommended Workloads

Level 1: One set of 2 to 4 repetitions, to start

Level 2: One set of 10 to 15 repetitions

Level 3: Set 1—10 repetitions with half the amount of resistance used in set 2

        Set 2—10 repetitions maximum

        Set 3—15 to 20 repetitions maximum

Grab the upper handles of the machine and pull them down until your arms and body form a Y.

lower portions of the chest, contributing to a full-bosomed look. (If you vary this workout by bending from the hips while maintaining the normal arch in your spine, you work the middle chest, further contributing to the desired results.)

PUSH-UP
(for the Entire Chest)

Weight machines, cable machines, dumbbells and other modern-day bodybuilding gadgetry aside, the good old-fashioned Push-Up still has a place in development of the chest. Full

Inhale slightly and pull the handles down until your hands are crossed in front of your hips. Lean slightly forward (about 20 degrees). Hold for a second, then exhale as you allow the handles to return to the position from which you started. Repeat.

PUSH-UP (FULL OR HALF)

Recommended Workloads

Level 1: One set of 2 to 3 repetitions, to start
Level 2: One set of 8 to 10 repetitions
Level 3: One set of 8 repetitions plus one set of 10 to 15 repetitions

Begin in the raised position, with your arms and body straight.

Lower yourself, keeping your trunk straight, until your chest lightly touches the floor. Raise yourself up until your arms are once again straight. Repeat.

Push-Ups (see the opposite page), done with the hands placed shoulder-width apart (fingers pointing inward, elbows outward), are best for the mid- chest. This ensures that maximum work will be done by the pectoral muscles of the chest as opposed to the tricep muscles at the back of the upper

To do easier Push-Ups, begin in the position shown, knees touching the floor and arms straight.

Inhale as you lower your chest to the floor. Your upper body should be rigid and straight. Return to the arms-straight position, exhaling after you pass the "sticking point"—that is, the hardest part of the return trip. Repeat.

arms. When performed in this way, Push-Ups are comparable to the Bench Press using dumbbells.

For the upper chest, keep your elbows in and your fingers pointed straight ahead.

If you're not yet strong enough to perform straight-leg Push-Ups, you can do half Push-Ups from your knees instead of your toes, as shown in the photos on page 79. Don't think of this variation as "cheating," though—your chest muscles are still doing a lot of work.

CHAPTER 8

THE SHOULDERS AND BACK

Perfect complements to a firmer bosom

Shirley was puzzled when I suggested she add Arm Raises and Lat Pull-Downs to her whole body reshaping program, to firm up her deltoids, trapezius and other muscles in the upper torso and back.

"Wait a minute, Dr. Yessis—I want to look fit, but not ferocious," said Shirley. "Won't developing my shoulder and back muscles make me look like a lumberjack?"

Shirley's concern was one I hear often from women who begin to work out. They assume that developing the muscles of their shoulders and back will make them look unfeminine. "I do want to improve the appearance of my chest," said Shirley. "But that's as far as I'll go in the area of my upper body."

"But developing your shoulders and back *will* help improve the appearance of your chest," I told Shirley. "A big part of having an attractive and prominent bustline is possessing the right posture and stamina to stand straight and tall, with your shoulders held back. Strong shoulder and back muscles can help you do that. Developing these muscles can also help you look more youthful by giving you the strength you need to keep from slouching, making the most of a well-developed chest."

I also mentioned that the exercises I was about to prescribe help women get rid of that annoying roll of fat that tends to accumulate beneath the shoulder blades, at the bra line.

Now Shirley was interested, but she still had some reservations. "You're sure I won't end up looking like Hulk Hogan?"

"No, you won't look like Hulk Hogan," I assured her. "You'll be strengthening and defining your shoulder and back muscles, but they won't substantially increase."

Almost as an afterthought, I told Shirley "Even if you do experience some muscular growth, it will only be to your advantage: Adding width to your shoulders would make your waist and hips look slimmer by comparison. You can wear backless sundresses with pride."

Shirley's enthusiasm grew. I also mentioned yet another benefit to exercising the muscles of the shoulders and back. "The exercises I'm going to suggest can do a great deal to relieve the pain and stiffness that tend to accumulate in the shoulder and neck

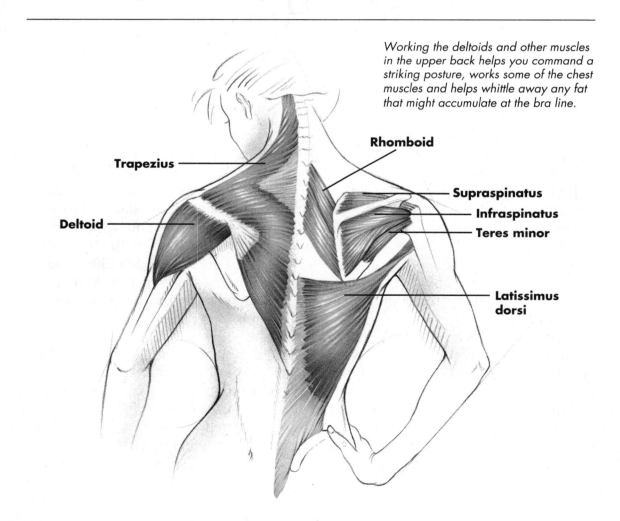

Working the deltoids and other muscles in the upper back helps you command a striking posture, works some of the chest muscles and helps whittle away any fat that might accumulate at the bra line.

Rhomboid

Trapezius

Supraspinatus

Infraspinatus

Deltoid

Teres minor

Latissimus dorsi

muscles after long periods of sitting or as a result of psychological stress," I told her. "By working these muscles, you'll be giving yourself your own internal massage."

Now Shirley was definitely psyched.

WORKING THE WHOLE TEAM

The exercises that follow develop specific shoulder and back muscles— namely, the deltoids, the rhomboids, the trapezius, the latissimus dorsi (or "lats," for short), the teres major and a deeper, specialized group of muscles collectively known as the rotator cuff, which forms the shoulder joint.

The shoulder and back muscles are a little more complicated than the chest muscles: They work as a well-organized team whose functions overlap but never conflict. This means that some of the following exercises will benefit more than one of the muscle groups of the shoulders and back at

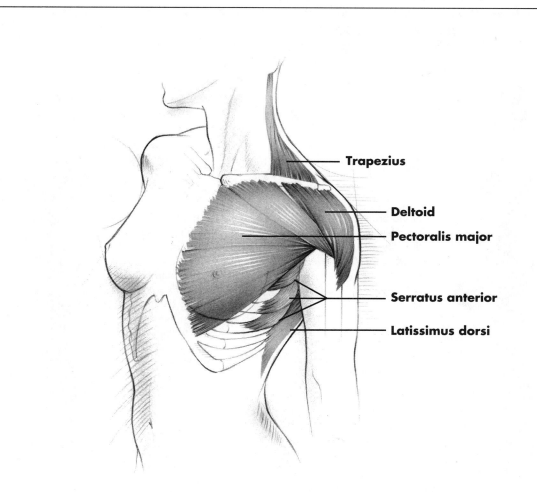

Trapezius

Deltoid

Pectoralis major

Serratus anterior

Latissimus dorsi

the same time. They also work the pectoralis minor (see the chest illustration on page 64) and the serratus anterior (at your sides). Since the exercises here incorporate all these muscles to some degree, shaping your back and shoulders plays a big role in achieving a toned and shapely "Barbie Doll" torso.

The exercises described here give the maximum workout in minimum time, contributing to a more shapely physique without compromising results.

FRONT ARM RAISE USING A STRENGTH BAR

Recommended Workloads

Level 1: One set of 3 to 4 repetitions, to start
Level 2: One set of 10 to 15 repetitions
Level 3: Set 1—10 repetitions with half the amount of weight used in set 2
Set 2—8 to 10 repetitions maximum
Set 3—15 to 20 repetitions maximum

Stand erect with your feet less than shoulder-width apart (left). Hold the strength bar at your thighs.

Keeping your arms relatively straight and your back as erect as possible, inhale and raise the strength bar overhead. Exhale as you return the strength bar to the starting position, and repeat.

FRONT ARM RAISE
(for the Front Deltoids
and Upper Chest)

Performed with a strength bar—a short barbell with a 5- to 10-pound weight at the center—this exercise (shown on the opposite page) is highly effective for developing the deltoids. (You may also perform Front Arm Raises using a 2- to 5-pound dumbbell.) Don't be overambitious, though: Too heavy a weight will force you to bend your arms and lift with your trunk, which is not your goal here. If

---

LATERAL ARM RAISE USING DUMBBELLS

Recommended Workloads

Level 1: One set of 3 to 5 repetitions, to start
Level 2: One set of 15 repetitions
Level 3: Set 1—10 repetitions with half the amount of weight used in set 2
Set 2—10 repetitions maximum
Set 3—15 to 20 repetitions maximum

Stand with your feet shoulder-width apart, holding a dumbbell at each side, as shown.

Inhale, then raise your arms sideways until you're holding the dumbbells directly overhead (or at least at a 45-degree angle, if you're just starting out). Exhale as you slowly lower the weights to your sides, and repeat.

Lateral Arm Raise Using a Lateral Shoulder Raise Machine

Recommended Workloads

Level 1: One set of 3 to 5 repetitions per arm, to start

Level 2: One set of 15 repetitions per arm

Level 3: Set 1—10 repetitions per arm with half the amount of resistance used in set 2

Set 2—7 to 10 repetitions per arm maximum

Set 3—15 to 20 repetitions per arm maximum

Position yourself as shown, resting your upper arms against the resistance pads and grasping the handles.

Inhale slightly and hold your breath as you raise your left arm until it forms a 45-degree angle with the horizontal, as shown. Exhale as you slowly return to the starting position, and repeat.

you can't keep your arms and back straight, try a lighter weight.

LATERAL ARM RAISE
(for the Middle Deltoids and Trapezius)

This exercise works the deltoids as well as the upper and lower parts of the trapezius, the muscle extending from the base of your skull to your lower back. It's excellent for shaping the middle of your upper back and relieving head and neck pain due to muscular tension caused by long periods of sitting or psychological stress.

You can perform this exercise using either dumbbells (see page 85) or a lateral shoulder raise machine (sometimes called a deltoid machine), commonly found in gyms.

As with the Front Arm Raise, it's important to start out with weights light enough to allow you to keep your arms and back relatively straight. For most women, dumbbells weighing 2 to 5 pounds each should be enough. This, too, is a case where more is definitely not better: If you use weights that are too heavy, you change the technique, and the exercise won't be as effective. (Plus you risk injury.)

To perform Lateral Arm Raises on a lateral shoulder raise machine, follow the instructions on the opposite page. (Doing Lateral Arm Raises on a weight machine is somewhat more taxing than the dumbbell version, so the recommended workload for Level 3 is slightly less with this version.)

You can also do both arms simultaneously. In that case, raise your arms to shoulder height but not much higher.

REVERSE FLY
(for the Back of the Deltoids, the Rhomboids and the Middle of the Trapezius)

This is an excellent exercise for developing the muscles responsible for helping you to maintain good (and flattering) shoulders-back, chest-out posture. Flies are best performed on a bench high enough to keep the dumbbells from contacting the floor (see page 88), but even a lower one will do. Just allow the weights to rest on the floor with your arms spread wide.

As with Front and Lateral Arm Raises, this exercise does not require heavy weights to be effective. One- to 5-pound dumbbells should be enough at the start. If you proceed up to heavier weights, it's safer and more effective to perform this exercise with your legs straddling the bench, with the balls of your feet on the floor.

LAT PULL-DOWN
(for the Latissimus Dorsi and Teres Major)

In advanced bodybuilders, the latissimus dorsi look like the "wings" on a flying squirrel. They give the back an impressive appearance of breadth, especially when flexed. You needn't develop the lats to this degree, however. By combining these exercises

(continued on page 91)

REVERSE FLY USING DUMBBELLS

Recommended Workloads

Level 1: One set of 2 to 3 repetitions, to start
Level 2: One set of 10 to 12 repetitions
Level 3: Set 1—10 repetitions with half the amount of weight used in set 2
Set 2—8 to 10 repetitions maximum
Set 3—15 to 20 repetitions maximum

Lie facedown on a narrow, padded weight bench, holding dumbbells with palms facing in, as shown.

Take a moderately deep breath, then raise your arms until they align with your shoulders, to start. (Eventually, you should be able to raise the weights higher, which is even more effective.) Exhale as you slowly lower the weights to the starting position, then repeat.

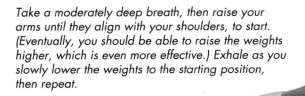

LAT PULL-DOWN USING A WIDE GRIP

Recommended Workloads

Level 1: One set of 2 to 3 repetitions, to start
Level 2: One set of 10 to 15 repetitions
Level 3: Set 1—10 repetitions with half the amount of resistance used in set 2
        Set 2—8 to 10 repetitions maximum
        Set 3—15 to 20 repetitions maximum

Adjust the seat and secure your thighs so that when you sit on the bench, you can hold the bar with your arms outstretched, as shown.

Inhale and lean forward slightly, and pull the bar down until it lightly touches the top of your shoulders and the base of your neck, as shown. Do not bend your neck forward. (If this is too difficult, pull the bar down to your upper chest instead.) Exhale as you gradually allow the bar to return to its starting position, then repeat.

LAT PULL-DOWN USING A NARROW GRIP

Recommended Workloads

Level 1: One set of 2 to 3 repetitions, to start
Level 2: One set of 10 to 15 repetitions
Level 3: Set 1—10 repetitions with half the amount of resistance used in set 2
         Set 2—8 to 10 repetitions maximum
         Set 3—15 to 20 repetitions maximum

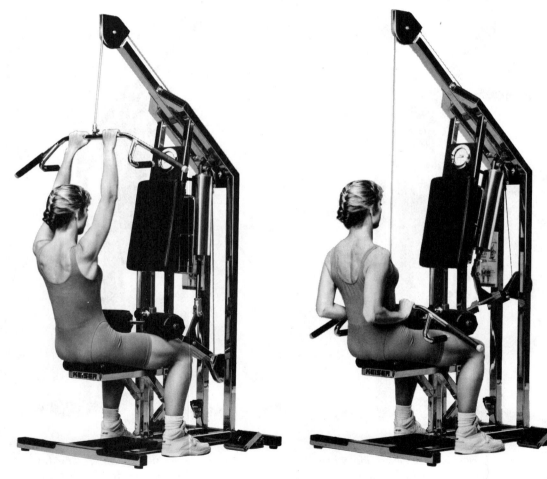

Again, secure your thighs on the bench, as shown, and grip the bar with your hands just a few inches away from the center point.

Inhale and lower the bar to your stomach, as shown. (If you have problems pulling the bar all the way to your stomach, lean back as you pull.) Gradually allow the bar to return to the starting position, then repeat.

(which strengthen and tone these very large muscles at each side of the upper back and most of the lower back) with the abdominal exercises in chapter 10, you will firm and shape your entire torso. As a side benefit, you'll also help protect yourself against lower back injury, since one of the functions of the lower portion of the lats is to help support the spine.

SHOULDER SHRUG USING DUMBBELLS

Recommended Workloads

Level 1: One set of 3 to 4 repetitions, to start
Level 2: One set of 10 to 12 repetitions
Level 3: Set 1—10 repetitions with half the amount of weight used in set 2
　　　　　Set 2—8 to 10 repetitions maximum
　　　　　Set 3—15 to 20 repetitions maximum

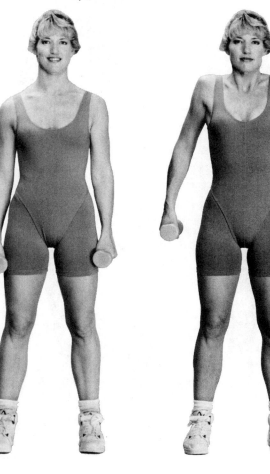

Stand with your feet shoulder-width apart, holding dumbbells at your sides.

Inhale slightly, then raise your shoulders as close to your ears as possible, as shown. Hold for a few seconds. Exhale as you lower your shoulders to the starting position, then repeat.

Performing the Lat Pull-Down with a wide grip (shown on page 89) works the upper part of the lats; a narrow grip (shown on page 90) works the lower lats. For full development of this muscle, I therefore recommend alternating between the two: Do one set using a narrow grip and then another set using a wider one.

To perform this exercise, you'll

OVERHEAD PRESS USING DUMBBELLS

Recommended Workloads

Level 1: One set of 2 to 4 repetitions, to start
Level 2: One set of 10 to 15 repetitions
Level 3: Set 1—10 repetitions with half the amount of weight used in set 2
Set 2—8 to 10 repetitions maximum
Set 3—15 to 20 repetitions maximum

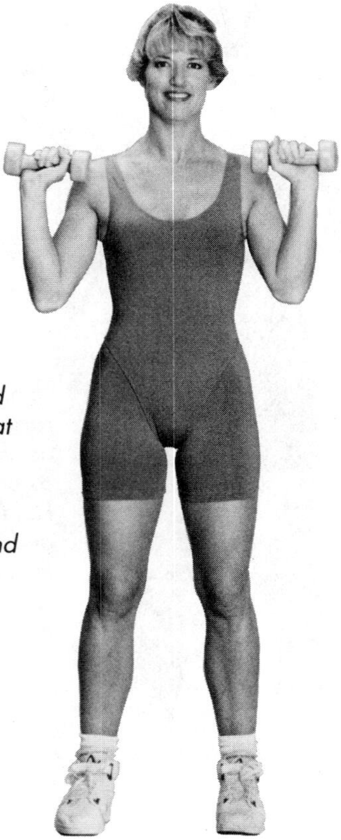

Stand straight and hold the weights at shoulder height, palms facing forward and elbows out to the sides and back, as shown.

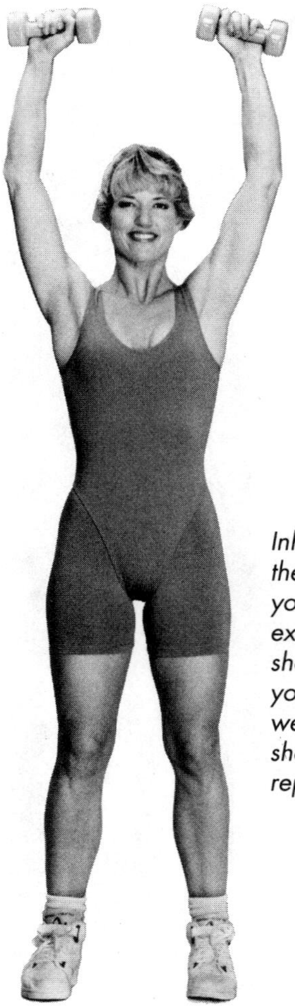

Inhale, then raise the dumbbells until your arms are fully extended, as shown. Exhale as you lower the weights to your shoulders, then repeat.

need access to what's known as a lat or pull-down machine. (Don't worry if the machine you use doesn't have the extra grips shown in the photos; they're for a different kind of exercise.)

SHOULDER SHRUG (for the Trapezius)

Rounded, stooped shoulders do nothing to flatter your bosom, shoul-

(continued on page 97)

If you prefer, you can also perform Overhead Presses using a neutral grip, with elbows forward, as shown.

OVERHEAD PRESS USING A BARBELL

Recommended Workloads

Level 1: One set of 2 to 4 repetitions, to start

Level 2: One set of 10 to 15 repetitions

Level 3: Set 1—10 repetitions with half the amount of weight used in set 2

Set 2—8 to 10 repetitions maximum

Set 3—15 to 20 repetitions maximum

Inhale and raise the barbell overhead, as shown. Exhale and lower the bar to your chest, then repeat.

Stand with your feet shoulder-width apart and hold the barbell at chest level, as shown.

OVERHEAD PRESS USING AN OVERHEAD PRESS MACHINE

Recommended Workloads

Level 1: One set of 2 to 4 repetitions, to start
Level 2: One set of 10 to 15 repetitions
Level 3: Set 1—10 repetitions with half the amount of resistance used in set 2
Set 2—8 to 10 repetitions maximum
Set 3—15 to 20 repetitions maximum

Adjust the seat so that you can grasp the resistance handles at approximately shoulder level, as shown.

Inhale and push the resistance handles until your arms are fully extended, as shown. Exhale as you return to the starting position, and repeat.

BENT-OVER DUMBELL ROW

Recommended Workloads

Level 1: One set of 3 to 4 repetitions per arm, to start

Level 2: One set of 10 to 15 repetitions per arm

Level 3: Set 1—10 repetitions per arm with half the amount of weight used in set 2

Set 2—8 to 10 repetitions per arm maximum

Set 3—15 to 20 repetitions per arm maximum

Kneel against one end of a padded weight bench with your left knee, keeping your right leg slightly bent, as shown. Support yourself with your left arm and hold a dumbbell with your right hand, as shown. Keep your back slightly arched.

Inhale and lift the dumbbell until your right elbow is a few inches higher than your back, as shown. Remember to keep your back slightly arched and your support leg straight. Exhale and return the dumbbell to the start position, and repeat.

ders or back. This exercise (see page 91) works the upper trapezius muscle (running from the back of your neck to your upper back) and is great for developing square, statuesque shoulders. (Use 2- to 5-pound dumbbells.)

OVERHEAD PRESS
(for the Upper and Lower Trapezius plus the Middle and Front Deltoids)

Traditionally known as a military press, the Overhead Press is an oldie but still a very goodie and can be done with dumbbells, a single barbell or a weight machine.

If you opt to use dumbbells, 5 pounds should be about right. Start with the instructions on page 92. For variety, you can also do this exercise by raising and lowering the weights behind your head, with your elbows held out to the sides and slightly back. For yet another variation, you can do the exercise in an alternating fashion, raising the weights in front of your head, first with the elbows forward and then with them out to the sides.

If you want to try a barbell for the Overhead Press (see page 94), a bar weighing anywhere from 10 to 15 pounds should suffice. As with the dumbbell version, you can try lowering the bar behind your head (with elbows out) or to the chest (with elbows in). Or you can alternate between the front and back. (This takes considerably more flexibility, however).

You can also perform Overhead Presses on an overhead press machine (see page 95). Start easy, and don't use weights that are too heavy—if you have to strain, you risk compacting your spine.

BENT-OVER DUMBBELL ROW
(for the Lower Lats and Related Muscles)

Here's another torso-toning basic that works a number of shoulder and back muscles—the lower latissimus dorsi, the teres major, the rear deltoids, the mid-trapezius and the rhomboids—in one fell swoop. Use a 2- to 5-pound dumbbell. Do one set with your right arm, as shown on the opposite page, then switch positions and do a set with the left arm, using the opposite leg for support.

CHAPTER 9

❖

THE UPPER ARMS
A shape-up program for well-toned arms

From what I hear around the gym, more and more women seem to be concerned about the appearance of their arms. Not too long ago, for example, I overheard a woman in her early thirties saying that she wished she had the arms of rock star/pin-up girl Madonna, to which her friend responded that she, in turn, coveted the arms of Linda Hamilton (à la *Terminator 2*). Can you imagine that conversation taking place a few years ago? I certainly can't.

What seems to bother women most is flabbiness at the back of the upper arms, a condition I've heard referred to derogatorily as "jiggly fat" or "bat wings." The fat in this area sags for one simple reason: There's too much fat and not enough muscle. What's

more, untoned muscles can sometimes appear as loose as fat itself. So fat-burning (aerobic) exercise and a low-fat diet can do only so much to whittle away bat wing arm flab. To seek real improvement in this area, you have to tone the arm muscles, especially the triceps (on the back of your upper arms).

This "saggy muscle" phenomenon can occur anywhere on the body, of course, but it seems to happen most often with the arms, given how most women avoid arm exercises. They work to tighten the muscles of their hips, waist and thighs until they're blue in the face but avoid working their arms for fear of developing "unfeminine" muscular bulk.

If this is a concern of yours, please

put it aside. Building considerable muscular bulk requires the male hormone testosterone, which you're very unlikely to have to any significant degree. You'll develop firmer and stronger arms by doing the exercises described here, but your arms will not become appreciably larger. In fact, if your arms are a little too big for your taste, they may very well become smaller, especially if you follow the Body Shaping Diet and combine

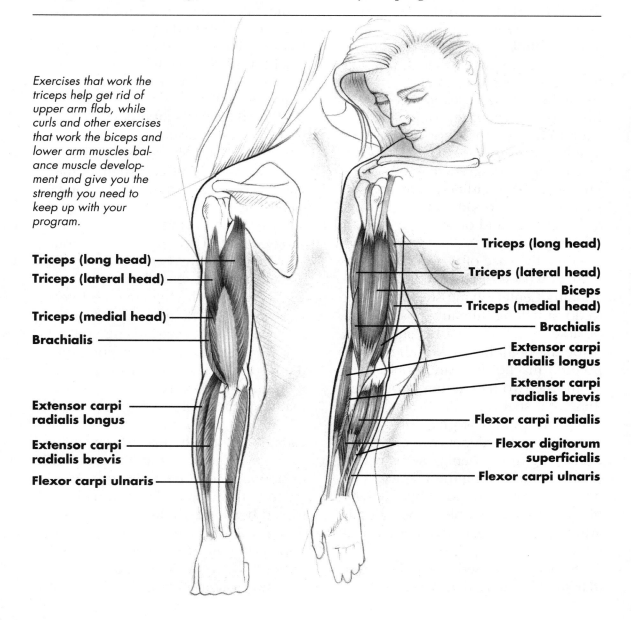

Exercises that work the triceps help get rid of upper arm flab, while curls and other exercises that work the biceps and lower arm muscles balance muscle development and give you the strength you need to keep up with your program.

Triceps (long head)

Triceps (lateral head)

Triceps (medial head)

Brachialis

Extensor carpi radialis longus

Extensor carpi radialis brevis

Flexor carpi ulnaris

Triceps (long head)

Triceps (lateral head)

Biceps

Triceps (medial head)

Brachialis

Extensor carpi radialis longus

Extensor carpi radialis brevis

Flexor carpi radialis

Flexor digitorum superficialis

Flexor carpi ulnaris

toning exercises with regular aerobic workouts.

SHAPELIER *AND* STRONGER

I always advise women to include at least some arm-toning exercises in their Body Shaping workouts. There's no better way to "bag the sag" of the all-too-troublesome upper arm area—or to prevent slack muscle tone in the first place—than to firm and strengthen the muscles in this area. But appearance aside, some women want to firm up their upper arms for purely practical purposes: They want to build up their strength—to lift carry-on luggage into airline overhead compartments, board-sail, heft 25 pounds of cat litter in and out of their cars and so forth.

Take the case of Sharon, a young woman who walked into the Sports Training Center saying she was ready to do "anything humanly possible" to be able to deliver on a bet she had made the night before with her 180-pound, "macho" husband Ron. It seems the two had gotten into something of a spat regarding Ron's claim that Sharon's lack of physical strength was making her dependent on him for everything from opening stubborn pickle jars to cutting the grass, to which Sharon responded by betting him $100 she'd be able to beat him in arm wrestling if he'd give her a year to train.

Sharon confessed to me, however, that she had more than a silly arm

wrestling competition on her mind when she made the wager. "I decided I wanted to be stronger for a lot of reasons," she said. "Say there was an emergency with the kids, or I got a flat tire out in the middle of nowhere, or some creep gave me a hard time on the street. I wanted to be stronger not just to make my husband swallow his macho pride but for the safety of my children and for my own independence as well."

I liked Sharon's attitude: determined, but still distinctly feminine. So we got to work. Sharon worked as hard as anyone I've seen here at the Sports Training Center. In fact, she became something of an inspiration for all of us. Within several months, she progressed to Level 3 in her workouts, and afterward, she continued to push herself hard but sensibly.

Then came the big day: the Kitchen Table Arm Wrestling Match with her husband. I don't mind telling you I was all pins and needles waiting for the results, which Sharon shared with me none too nonchalantly by phone that very evening.

"I did it, I beat him," she exclaimed. "Not only that," she continued excitedly, "but he wanted to go double or nothing, and I beat him *again!*"

In her estimation, Sharon had tripled her strength. Rest assured, though: Sharon's arms had *not* grown appreciably in size. To be sure, her upper arms were significantly firmer and more muscularly defined but not larger—something she had not thought possible when we first discussed the training she would need to do. In fact, a year of working out had actually *trimmed her down* more than it had bulked her up. As a bonus, she had lost an inch from her waist and two inches from her hips, thanks to the extra calories her workouts had burned plus some wise changes she had made in her diet.

Sharon was extremely happy with her new physique. And so was her husband.

"Ron now describes me as 'lean and just a little bit mean,'" Sharon told me the day after her victory. "Better yet, he doesn't seem to have any hard feelings about the arm wrestling match. The other morning he was so cute—he asked if I'd open a jar of wheat germ for him. He was starting a Body Shaping program of his own and wanted to eat before heading off to the gym. He (gulp!) wants a rematch in six months!"

As Sharon discovered, developing greater arm strength doesn't mean sacrificing femininity. Quite the contrary, it can help "solidify" that femininity by providing the strength, independence and confidence sometimes needed to define and defend it. Let's look now at the muscles and the exercises that can help you do just that.

"LITING" OFF THE FLAB

The upper arms are made up of the three major muscle groups—the bi-ceps and brachialis (located at the front of the upper arm) and the triceps (at the back of the upper arm).

The exercises that follow are designed to tone up the triceps and biceps—the reason being that muscle development should be well balanced for you to look and perform well. Activities such as changing a tire or hefting luggage overhead require strength from all your upper (and lower) arm muscles, not just an isolated group. And of course, from a strictly cosmetic point of view, this will give you a better-proportioned look.

BICEPS CURL
(for the Front of the Upper Arms)

This is one of the oldest and most basic muscle-toning exercises, but it does the job. To perform curls, you can use dumbbells (shown on page 102), a barbell or a weight machine. The technique is essentially the same and will achieve the same effects.

When doing this exercise, it's important to fully extend your arms while in the "rest" (return) position, to prevent your biceps and brachialis muscles from becoming short and tight. Also, don't thrust your pelvis forward to help you heft the weights up with each repetition, as doing so would minimize the effectiveness of this exercise. In fact, you may want to stand with your buttocks, shoulders and elbows against a wall when doing curls, to help resist this tendency. Then

(continued on page 104)

BICEPS CURL USING DUMBBELLS

Recommended Workloads

Level 1: One set of 3 to 4 repetitions per arm, to start

Level 2: One set of 15 to 20 repetitions per arm

Level 3: Set 1—10 repetitions per arm with half the amount of weight used in set 2

Set 2—8 to 10 repetitions per arm maximum

Set 3—15 to 20 repetitions per arm maximum

Stand in a well-balanced position with your feet shoulder-width apart. Hold the dumbbells with your hands held shoulder-width apart, palms facing inward and arms fully extended so that your hands rest alongside your upper thighs, as shown.

Inhale and raise the right dumbbell with a turn of the hand so that the palm is facing up. Continue the raise until your elbow is bent at slightly less than a 90-degree angle. Be sure to keep your upper arms close to your sides, as shown. Begin to exhale as you slowly lower the dumbbell to the initial position at your thighs, in a controlled return. Then repeat with the left arm.

FRENCH PRESS USING A SINGLE DUMBBELL

Recommended Workloads

Level 1: One set of 3 to 4 repetitions, to start

Level 2: One set of 10 to 15 repetitions

Level 3: Set 1—10 repetitions with half the amount of weight used in set 2
Set 2—8 to 10 repetitions maximum
Set 3—15 to 20 repetitions maximum

Stand with your feet shoulder-width apart. Hold a dumbbell overhead with your arms fully extended, as shown.

Inhale as you now slowly lower the dumbbell behind your head as far as possible, keeping your elbows pointed upward, as shown. When you've reached this bottom position, do not pause. Instead, begin to raise the dumbbell immediately so that your arms are once again extended, exhaling after you've passed the most difficult point of the return lift. Pause for a second or so, and repeat.

in order to get maximum benefit from the exercise, your buttocks, shoulders and elbows should remain in contact with the wall throughout the entire lift. After you learn the correct elbow posi- tion, you can stand free of the wall.

If you're starting out, it's best to begin with about 4 to 10 pounds of weight total (2 to 5 pounds each if you're using dumbbells, which are

TRICEPS PUSH-DOWN USING A PULLEY MACHINE

Recommended Workloads

Level 1: One set of 3 to 4 repetitions, to start
Level 2: One set of 15 to 20 repetitions
Level 3: Set 1—10 repetitions with half the amount of resistance used in set 2
  Set 2—8 to 10 repetitions maximum
  Set 3—15 to 20 repetitions maximum

Stand against the triceps push-down machine with your back against the sup- port, as shown. Grasp the pulley bar or grips with your palms facing downward and your arms bent at slightly less than a 90-degree angle. Your elbows should be tucked in as close as pos- sible to your body.

Inhale as you push down- ward and straighten your arms. Be sure to keep your elbows in at your sides, as shown. When your arms are almost fully extended (a position approximately 10 degrees short of a full extension is best), exhale and return to the starting position. Repeat.

more effective than barbells).

If you're doing this exercise with dumbbells, you can increase the effectiveness by holding the dumbbells with the palms facing inward, toward the thighs. Then as you raise the dumbbells, turn the palms faceup as your arms approach a 90-degree angle and higher. Lower, and repeat. This engages the biceps in both actions.

FRENCH PRESS
(for the Back of the Upper Arms, or Triceps)

Curls are great for toning the biceps and brachialis (the front of the upper arms), but they do nothing for the triceps (the all-important, flab-prone back of the upper arms). The French Press is a great exercise for toning this area. The easiest way to do this exercise is to use a single dumbbell weighing approximately 5 to 15 pounds (see page 103).

If for some reason you feel pain in your elbows when doing the French Press, substitute the Triceps Push-Down, which follows.

TRICEPS PUSH-DOWN
(for the Back of the Upper Arms)

This exercise uses a pulley machine and is also good for toning the triceps (see the opposite page). Most pulley machines have a short bar or angled grips. Set the pin at 5 to 20 pounds of resistance.

Variation: To work a slightly different portion of the triceps muscle,

you can also perform this exercise with less weight, holding the bar or grips with the palms facing upward or at an angle.

TRICEPS KICKBACK
(for the Uppermost Portion of the Back of the Upper Arms)

Yet another great exercise for the triceps—and especially for the uppermost segment of this muscle—is the Triceps Kickback (see page 106). This requires a bit more stability, balance and coordination to perform. And it's important to keep your back in a horizontal position when performing this exercise, to avoid injury and ensure that your muscles work against gravity for maximum resistance and effectiveness. It's best to work up to this exercise after mastering the French Press and Triceps Push-Down.

WRIST CURL AND REVERSE WRIST CURL
(for the Forearms)

Strong forearms may not be high on the wish list of many women, but they can sure come in handy for dealing with stubborn pickle jars and the like. Here are two excellent exercises that should substantially strengthen your forearms and hence gripping strength. As a bonus, strong forearm muscles are your best protection against the agonies of carpal tunnel syndrome, an increasingly common complaint among office workers who work at computer keyboards and others who perform repetitive motions with their hands.

We'll look at the Wrist Curl first (see page 108). Start with dumbbells of 2 to 3 pounds each and work up to 5 pounds or more.

While the Wrist Curl works the in-side (flexor) muscles of the forearms, you should also work the outside (extensor) muscles in order to avoid overdeveloping one set of muscles with neglect for a companion group. As with the Wrist Curl, you can perform this forearm exercise—the Re-

---

Triceps Kickback Using Dumbbells

Recommended Workloads

Level 1: One set of 3 to 4 repetitions per arm
Level 2: One set of 15 to 20 repetitions per arm
Level 3: Set 1—10 repetitions per arm with half the amount of weight used in set 2
Set 2—8 to 10 repetitions per arm maximum
Set 3—15 to 20 repetitions per arm maximum

Stand alongside a standard weight-training bench, bend at the hips, and grasp one end for support, as shown. In your other hand, hold a light (2- to 5-pound) dumbbell at your side with your arm bent and your palm facing inward.

Inhale slightly and extend your arm backward until it's straight, as shown. Hold your elbow close to your body.

Pause for a moment, then continue to move your arm backward and upward in an arc, keeping it as straight as possible for maximum results. The final position you reach should be well above the level of your back, as shown. Don't swing the weight. Exhale as you slowly lower your arm to the starting point. Repeat.

verse Wrist Curl—with dumbbells, beginning with approximately 2 to 5 pounds of weight (see page 110).

The greater the range of motion you can achieve in doing this exercise, the more strength and flexibility you'll gain. If you find your range of motion is quite limited (considerably less than what's shown in the photos), you may be using too much weight, which in turn prompts you to grasp the weight too tightly. If that's the case, use less weight and loosen your grip—you'll get greater results from the exercise.

WRIST CURL USING DUMBBELLS

Recommended Workloads

Level 1: One set of 4 to 5 repetitions, to start

Level 2: One set of 15 to 20 repetitions

Level 3: Set 1—10 repetitions with half the amount of weight used in set 2

Set 2—10 to 15 repetitions maximum

Set 3—20 repetitions maximum

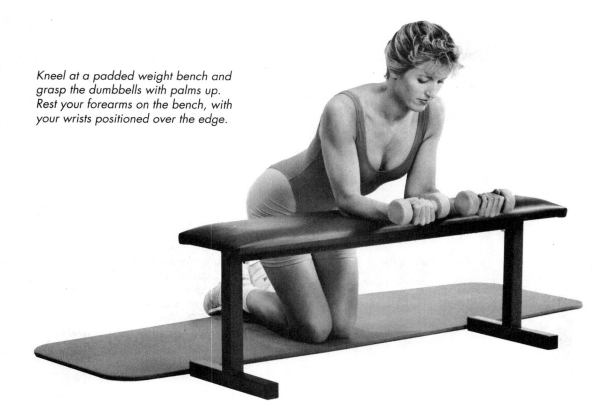

Kneel at a padded weight bench and grasp the dumbbells with palms up. Rest your forearms on the bench, with your wrists positioned over the edge.

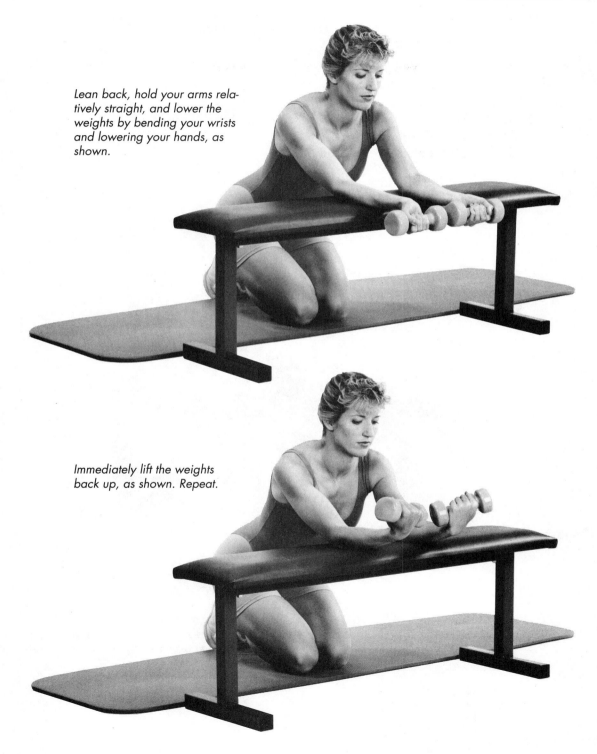

Lean back, hold your arms relatively straight, and lower the weights by bending your wrists and lowering your hands, as shown.

Immediately lift the weights back up, as shown. Repeat.

REVERSE WRIST CURL USING DUMBBELLS

Recommended Workloads

Level 1: One set of 4 to 5 repetitions, to start
Level 2: One set of 15 to 20 repetitions
Level 3: Set 1—10 repetitions with half the amount of weight used in set 2
　　　　　Set 2—10 to 15 repetitions maximum
　　　　　Set 3—20 repetitions maximum

As with the Wrist Curl, kneel at a padded weight bench. But this time, grasp the dumbbells with your palms facing down, as shown. Your arms should be bent at approximately a 90-degree angle, and your hands should extend over the edge of the bench so that they're free to move.

As with the Wrist Curl, lower the dumbbells as far as you can, keeping your forearms in firm contact with the bench and bending at the wrist.

Immediately lift the weights as high as you can without raising your forearms off the bench, as shown. Do this at a moderate pace. Inhale as you raise the dumbbells, and exhale as you lower them.

CHAPTER 10

❖

THE WAIST AND ABDOMEN

Tummy tighteners and waist whittlers that work the midsection

From the rib-crushing corsets of the nineteenth century to today's equally unfriendly belt vibrators, body wraps and gut-buster gizmos, there's never been a shortage of quick fixes promising to produce a flat stomach and washboard abdomen. Men and women alike bemoan their potbellies and love handles.

At this point, I have to set one thing straight: The stomach is an internal organ that you cannot "flatten." (Nor would you want to!) Granted, the stomach has its own set of muscles that contract when you digest food. But no amount of exercise will change these muscles, nor do they have any bearing on the appearance of your abdomen.

What people really mean when they say they want to "flatten their stomach" or "get rid of their potbelly" is that they need to firm up the abdominals ("abs"), muscles responsible for moving the trunk and spine, not for aiding digestion. The tighter the abs, the less the internal organs (including the stomach) protrude. But let's call an ab an ab, not a stomach.

In women who've borne children especially, the muscles of the abdomen stretch during pregnancy, and the internal organs within tend to bulge forward. Granted, getting rid of the layer of fat that tends to accumulate over these muscles plays a big part, and so getting rid of excess body fat (through diet and aerobics) is a step in the right direction. But don't make the mistake of ignoring the muscle part of the equation.

TIGHTER ABS

Tightening the abs and lower back muscles creates something of a muscular "corset" for the waist, front *and* back, getting rid of bothersome love handles and the so-called potbelly. Strengthening the abs also takes pressure off the spine, helping to combat swayback, a condition that can cause not just a protruding abdomen but lower back pain as well.

Perhaps you've already tried sit-ups

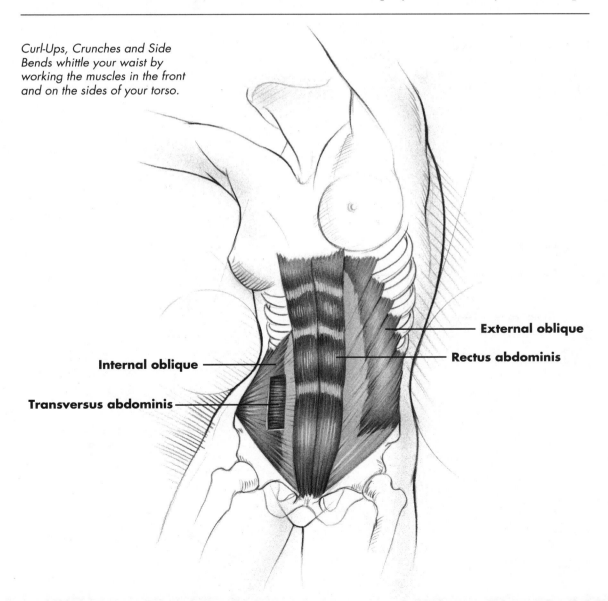

Curl-Ups, Crunches and Side Bends whittle your waist by working the muscles in the front and on the sides of your torso.

External oblique

Rectus abdominis

Internal oblique

Transversus abdominis

but found them difficult, tiresome or unproductive. Or maybe, like a lot of folks, you have a history of lower back trouble and shy away from anything that could aggravate the problem.

If sit-ups don't seem to pay off for you, perhaps you're not doing them correctly. They're a very effective exercise for firming the upper portion of the abdominal wall, the rectus abdominis (see the illustration on page 113) especially. If you have back problems, see a qualified medical expert. Done correctly, there is no reason sit-ups should put undue stress on the lower spine.

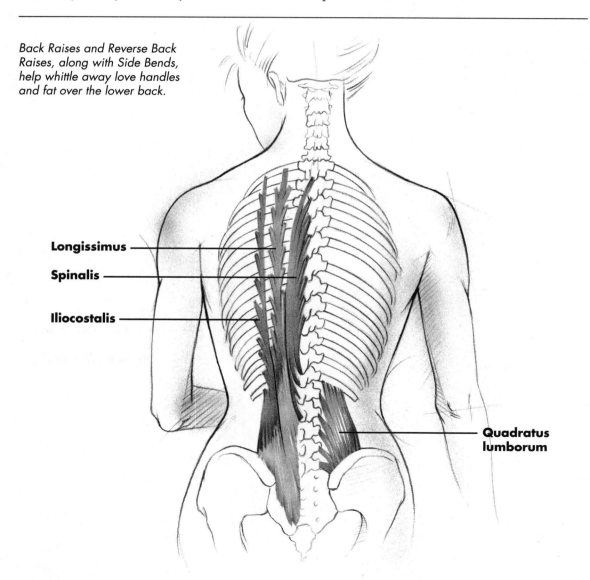

Back Raises and Reverse Back Raises, along with Side Bends, help whittle away love handles and fat over the lower back.

Longissimus

Spinalis

Iliocostalis

Quadratus lumborum

But even when done correctly, sit-ups alone can do only so much for your waistline. For a firmer and trimmer midsection, you also need to do exercises for the sides and back of your waist. Think about it: The waist is, after all, a 360-degree affair. Over the years, pounds can (and do) mount up at every angle.

That said, let's look at the best all-round exercises for trimming and firming the waist.

WHITTLE AWAY THAT SPARE TIRE

If you've been doing abdominal exercises with little success, the problem could be that you're not getting to all of the "plys" of which your "spare tire" is made. There is not just one abdominal muscle, you see, but four, each having its own particular functions and hence needing its own exercises for enacting these functions. (See the illustration on page 113.)

Outermost of these muscles is the rectus abdominis, which covers the front of the abdominal area and extends from the lower part of the rib cage all the way down to the pubic bone. Beneath the rectus abdominis and off to its sides are the external obliques, and beneath these are the internal obliques. They work with the rectus abdominis to move your trunk.

Deepest of the four abdominal muscles is the transversus abdominis, the number one muscle for holding in the abdominal organs. (During child-

birth, the obliques and transversus ab-domimis work together to enable women to exhale and push during de-livery—the rectus abdominis does not play a role.)

But enough anatomy. It's time to see how to pull these abdominal mus-cles into the kind of shape needed to reconfigure the waist.

CURL-UP (for the Upper Abdomen)

This exercise targets the rectus ab-dominis and is excellent for firming the upper area of the abdomen.

Curl-Ups done with the legs bent have been criticized for working the flexor muscles of the hips more so than the muscles of the abdomen, but in my view, the fuss has been much ado about nothing. Yes, bent-knee Curl-Ups do involve the hip flexors. But this should be considered a ben-efit, because well-developed hip flexors are important for proper align-ment of the pelvis, and they help tone the muscles of the hip area. Mean-while, the abdominal muscles still get the lion's share of the workout.

Also, many other fitness experts strongly advise against anchoring the feet, because that, too, involves the hip flexors. Again, I take exception to that point of view. I feel that devel-oping the hip flexors is needed, since these muscles work together in many activities, including walking, running, jumping, kicking and the like. Never-theless, if you've had any kind of

Curl-Up with Legs Bent

Recommended Workloads

Level 1: One set of 4 to 5 repetitions, to start
Level 2: One set of 15 to 20 repetitions
Level 3: One set of 20 repetitions plus one set of 20 to 30 repetitions

(1)

(2)

Lie on your back with your legs bent at the knees, your feet flat on the floor and your arms at your sides (1) or crossed over your chest (2).

Inhale slightly as you raise your head and shoulders off the floor. Concentrate on curling your trunk as much as possible, reaching a position 30 to 45 degrees from the floor if you can. Exhale and return to your starting position. Relax momentarily, and repeat.

lower back problems or sciatica pain, it's prudent to leave your feet unsecured or (better yet) check with a qualified orthopedist about the best technique for you.

This exercise (see the opposite page) and the modified versions that follow are best done on an exercise mat or a soft carpet. For beginners, keep your arms at your sides. If you're at Level 2, you may cross your arms over your chest—it's more difficult.

CRUNCH WITH FEET RAISED

Recommended Workloads

Level 1: One set of 4 to 5 repetitions, to start
Level 2: One set of 10 to 15 repetitions
Level 3: One set of 20 repetitions plus one set of 20 to 30 repetitions

Lie down with your feet propped up on a padded weight bench or chair and your arms crossed over your chest or placed at your sides.

Inhale and raise your head and shoulders to form a 20- to 30-degree angle with the floor. Then exhale and lower yourself all the way to the floor, to allow the abdominal muscles to relax momentarily. If you lower yourself only partway, your abdominals tend to shorten, which is not conducive to good upright posture and can lead to a rounded upper back.

MODIFIED CURL-UP (CRUNCH)
(for the Upper Abdomen)

If you find Curl-Ups too difficult, you can do a modified version, with your feet raised (see page 117). Descriptively known as the Crunch, this exercise also works the abdomen's upper section.

REVERSE SIT-UP
(for the Lower Abdomen)

Curl-Ups and Modified Curl-Ups (Crunches) do a great job of firming the upper part of the abdomen, but they do not do a good job of getting to the lower abdomen, an especially troublesome area for many women

REVERSE SIT-UP

Recommended Workloads

Level 1: One set of 4 to 5 repetitions, to start
Level 2: One set of 15 to 20 repetitions
Level 3: One set of 20 repetitions plus one set of 30 to 40 repetitions

Lie on your back with your arms at your sides, palms down.

To start, bend your knees and raise your legs so that your thighs are vertical, as shown.

Inhale slightly as you raise your pelvis off the floor and bring your knees to your chest. (When first doing this exercise, you may push down with your hands to help you get your hips off the floor and your knees as close as possible to your chest.) Then exhale as you return to your starting position. Rest for a second or two, then repeat. Do not, however, lower your feet to the floor until you've completed your set.

Once you become proficient at Reverse Sit-Ups done with your arms at your sides, you should do them with your arms stretched overhead, as shown in the next two photos, to give your lower abdominals the maximum workout.

(and particularly for those who've borne children).

The Reverse Sit-Up (see page 118) is great for reining in a protruding abdomen and correcting a potbelly. It also helps tighten the lower abdomen following childbirth. What's more, it can help minimize the distortion of these muscles that pregnancy causes in the first place.

Even if you haven't had children, Reverse Sit-Ups are among the best for tightening the abdominals, especially as you become proficient at them. This is because your range of motion will gradually increase, thus bringing into play more and more, and eventually all, of the muscles that comprise the abdominal wall. The exercise also stretches the lower back muscles very effectively, if you tend to have tight lower back muscles.

REVERSE TRUNK TWIST

Recommended Workloads

Level 1: 3 repetitions per side, to start

Level 2: 15 repetitions per side

Level 3: One set of 20 repetitions per side plus one set of 20 to 30 repetitions per side

Lie on your back with your arms out to the side, palms facing down. Keeping your legs straight or slightly bent at the knee and feet together, raise your thighs so that they form a 90-degree angle with the floor, as shown.

REVERSE TRUNK TWIST (for the Front and Sides of the Waist)

Curl-Ups work the upper abdomen, and Reverse Sit-Ups, the lower abdomen. But what can you do for those love handles at the sides of the abdomen? A trim and firm waist is a "full circle" affair, remember, so you also have to work the external and internal obliques, not just the muscles out front.

The answer is the Reverse Trunk Twist, shown on the opposite page. (Incidentally, this is *the* most effective exercise for achieving a flat abdomen.)

BACK RAISE (to Strengthen the Lower Back)

To fully work the midsection, it's important to develop the lower back muscles as well as the front and side muscles. Back Raises (see page 125)

Inhale slightly as you lower your legs to one side, keeping your feet together and maintaining a 90-degree angle, as shown. Keeping your arms and shoulders fully in contact with the floor, touch the floor with the outermost side of your lower foot.

Raise your legs back to a vertical position and exhale after you pass the most difficult part of the lift.

(continued)

work the spinalis, longissimus and ilio-costalis muscles (collectively known as the erector spinae) as well as some small, deeper muscles that hold the spine in place. So this exercise does double duty—it strengthens the back and helps prevent back pain.

The best way to do a Back Raise is to use a glute-ham developer (GHD), found in most gyms. If you don't have access to this equipment, you can do nearly as well with a sturdy table (such as a wooden picnic table) and someone to hold your legs. If you

---

REVERSE TRUNK TWIST — CONTINUED

Lower your legs in the opposite direction so that your lower foot again touches the floor.

Inhale and raise your legs back to the vertical, exhaling after you pass the most difficult part of the lift. Repeat.

REVERSE TRUNK TWIST WITH BENT KNEES

Recommended Workloads

Level 1: 3 repetitions per side, to start
Level 2: 15 repetitions per side
Level 3: One set of 20 repetitions per side plus one set of 20 to 30 repetitions per side

If you find the Reverse Trunk Twist too difficult at first, do this modified version: Bend your legs, as shown, or take your shoes off (or both). You can also ask someone to hold your shoulders if they have a tendency to rise from the floor. Eventually, you should be able to do the unmodified version, wearing shoes, with legs straight (or fairly straight, if you have tight hamstrings).

choose the table route, position your-self so that your trunk can hang over the edge of the table and your lower abdomen is supported by a rolled-up towel, for padding.

Caution: When doing Back Raises, proper positioning is very important. Your navel should be directly in line with or just slightly ahead of the for-ward-most edge of the padded seat on the GHD (or the edge of the table, if you're using a table).

It's also important to have your lower back rounded (flexed) before raising up, as the photo shows. Flexing the spine gives the lower back muscles a therapeutic stretch, which makes this exercise more effective as you rise up to a position in which your back be-comes slightly arched.

If you feel uncomfortable or disori-ented doing an exercise with your head upside down, you may want to skip the Back Raises and try the Re-verse Back Raises (which follow this group) instead.

REVERSE BACK RAISE
(for the Lower Back)

This exercise (shown on page 126) is similar to the Back Raise, except that you hang your lower body (hips and legs), not your trunk, over the seat of the GHD. If, as with Back Raises, you don't have access to a GHD and you're using a sturdy table of some kind, the table will have to be wide enough for you to grab on to the table's far edge or sides for support. (A solid wooden

picnic table would probably fill the bill.)

SIDE BEND
(for Love Handles, Abdominals and the Lower Back)

This unique exercise works not just the sides of the waist (the internal and external obliques) but also the rectus abdominis and the muscles of the lower back in one single motion. Side Bends are versatile; you can do them in any one of three ways—standing, lying on the floor or on a GHD.

To perform the standing Side Bend (shown on page 127), use a 5-, 10- or 15-pound dumbbell, depending on how far you advance.

The floor version of the Side Bend (shown on page 128) is more difficult than the standing technique, and you'll need an assistant to hold your legs. But it gives your obliques an even better workout.

Doing Side Bends using the GHD (shown on page 129) is a little more difficult. If you don't feel confident about this position, stick with the standing or floor version just described.

PELVIC THRUST
(for the Lower Back)

This is one of the easiest ways to strengthen your lower back—you don't need an assistant or special equipment. The Pelvic Thrust (shown on page 130) can also be used as a substitute for the Back Raise if you find it difficult.

BACK RAISE USING A GLUTE-HAM DEVELOPER

Recommended Workloads

Level 1: One set of 3 to 5 repetitions, to start
Level 2: One set of 15 to 20 repetitions
Level 3: One set of 20 repetitions plus one set of 25 to 30 repetitions

Starting position: Lie facedown with your feet secured beneath the rear pads and your pelvic girdle (the prominent bones at the front of your hips) resting on the padded seat, as shown. Cross your arms against your chest.

Inhale as you raise your trunk until your head and shoulders are higher than your legs, keeping your legs straight. Hold this position just briefly (a second or so). Then exhale as you gradually lower yourself back to the starting position. Relax for a moment, then repeat.

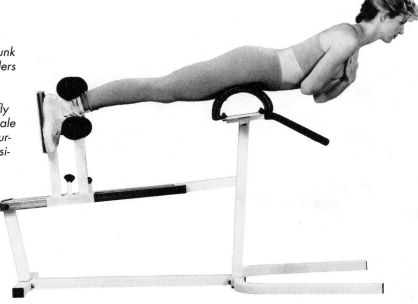

Reverse Back Raise Using a Glute-Ham Developer

Recommended Workloads

Level 1: One set of 5 to 6 repetitions, to start
Level 2: One set of 15 to 20 repetitions
Level 3: One set of 10 repetitions plus one set of 20 to 25 repetitions with ankle weights

Lean over the seat so that your abdomen is supported and your legs are at a 60-degree angle to the horizontal, as shown. To secure your head and shoulders, firmly grasp the rollers or back plate.

Inhale and raise your legs, as shown. (Try to raise them a bit higher than your back.) Then exhale and return slowly to your starting position. Repeat.

STANDING SIDE BEND

Recommended Workloads

Level 1: One set of 5 repetitions per side with a 5-pound dumbbell, to start

Level 2: One set of 10 repetitions per side with a 10-pound dumbbell

Level 3: One set of 10 repetitions per side with a 15-pound dumbbell plus one set of 20 repetitions per side with a 10-pound dumbbell

Stand with your legs about shoulder-width apart and hold a dumbbell in one hand.

Bend sideways, lowering the arm holding the dumbbell, as shown. Lean as far as possible without shifting your pelvis to the side.

When you've gone as far as you can go, inhale as you raise your trunk back to the erect position and exhale as you go over to the other side as far as possible. Inhale as you return to the erect position. Pause, and repeat.

SIDE BEND (FLOOR VERSION)

Recommended Workloads

Level 1: One set of 1 to 2 repetitions per side, to start
Level 2: One set of 5 to 10 repetitions per side
Level 3: One set of 15 to 20 repetitions per side

Lie on the floor on one side with someone sitting on your lower legs and holding your thighs, as shown. Cross your arms over your chest and hold your head in line with your trunk.

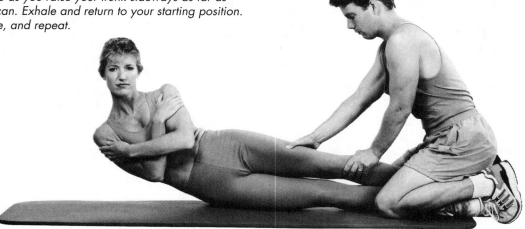

Inhale as you raise your trunk sideways as far as you can. Exhale and return to your starting position. Pause, and repeat.

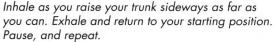

SIDE BEND USING A GLUTE-HAM DEVELOPER

Recommended Workloads

Level 1: One set of 1 to 2 repetitions per side, to start
Level 2: One set of 5 to 10 repetitions per side
Level 3: Two sets of 15 to 20 repetitions per side

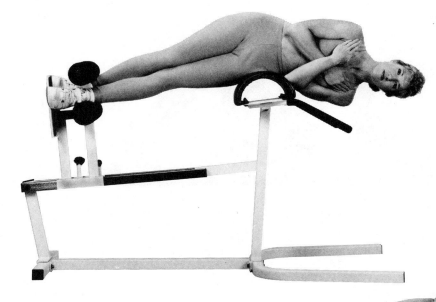

Position yourself on the GHD with your hips on the seat, as shown, and your arms crossed over your chest. Inhale as you lower your upper body as far as possible, then exhale.

Inhale and lift your upper body as far as possible, as shown. Then exhale slightly as you lower your trunk to the beginning position. Pause, then repeat.

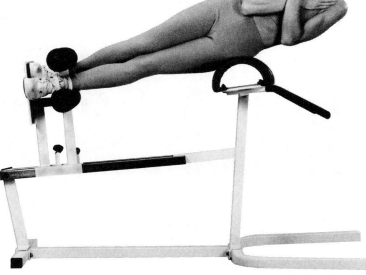

Pelvic Thrust

Recommended Workloads

Level 1: One set of 5 repetitions, to start
Level 2: One set of 10 to 15 repetitions
Level 3: Two sets of 20 to 30 repetitions

Lie on your back with your knees bent, feet flat on the floor and arms at your sides, palms down.

Inhale and raise your pelvis until there is a slight arch in your lower back. Lower your pelvis to the floor and exhale. Repeat.

CHAPTER 11

❖

THE HIPS
AND BUTTOCKS
Smaller jeans despite your genes

The guiding principle behind Body Shaping, as we've seen, is really very simple: You shape and tone muscles while you whittle away fat that may be keeping those muscles hidden from view. This can produce truly dramatic changes in the way you look, changes far more desirable than if you were to try to reduce fat by dieting only.

This two-pronged attack of muscle toning plus fat reduction can produce some very remarkable results in trouble zones such as the buttocks and hips especially—the shape of which many women consider to be cast in genetic concrete.

No way, you say? You have tried every exercise program to come down

the pike—jogging, donkey kicks, you name it—and haven't lost an inch around your hips?

All I can say to that is this: Three very specific muscles are responsible for giving the hips and buttocks their shape, and unless these muscles are exercised in precisely the right way, much effort can go for naught. Let's take a close look at what it takes to give these muscles the attention they really need.

MEET THE GLUTEUS FAMILY

It might help to think of your hip and buttock muscles as being like the layers of a three-layer cake. (See the illustration on page 132.) One "layer" is the gluteus maximus, the largest and outermost muscle of the three and the muscle most responsible for giving firmness and shape to the buttocks, or "rear."

Underneath and to the sides of the gluteus maximus lie the gluteus medius and gluteus minimus, the muscles most responsible for giving firmness and form to the hips. Perfecting the shape of the buttocks and hips, therefore, requires something of a "di-

vision of labor." You work each layer of the cake individually in order to get optimum results collectively. Serious bodybuilders have known that for years, which is why they go to such lengths to isolate the muscles of the hip and buttock region in their workouts. What's best for developing one muscle is not best for developing others, hence the need for a three-pronged attack.

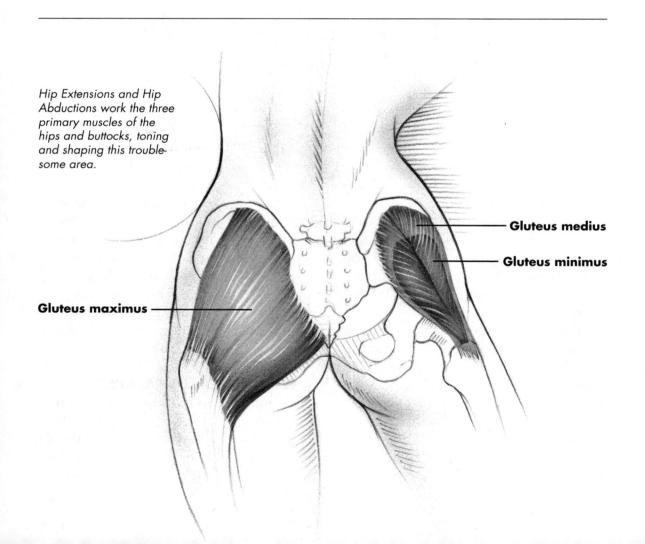

Hip Extensions and Hip Abductions work the three primary muscles of the hips and buttocks, toning and shaping this troublesome area.

Gluteus medius

Gluteus minimus

Gluteus maximus

DO'S AND DON'TS FOR WORKING THE GLUTEUS MAXIMUS

Though it may be best known for its relatively inactive function of providing something on which to sit, the gluteus maximus is one of the largest and potentially strongest muscles of the body. The uppermost portion of the muscle assists in moving the leg outward from the body, while the lower portion assists in pulling the leg inward. The muscle especially comes into play when moving the leg backward, hence the behind "donkey kicks" for working the backside.

Donkey kicks (shown below) rarely produce the desired results, however, because they do not provide any appreciable resistance for the gluteus maximus. Donkey kicks can even be dangerous because they can put a lot of strain on the lower back. If you raise and rotate the hips all in one mo-

Forget donkey kicks, shown here. Not only is this exercise ineffective, but it can strain the lower back and cause injury as well.

HIP EXTENSION USING A HIGH PULLEY MACHINE

Recommended Workloads

Level 1: One set of 2 to 5 repetitions per leg, to start
Level 2: One set of 15 to 20 repetitions per leg
Level 3: Set 1—10 repetitions per leg with half the amount of resistance used in set 2
Set 2—10 to 12 repetitions per leg maximum
Set 3—20 repetitions per leg maximum

Starting position: Stand facing the pulley machine with the cable strap attached to the ankle of the leg to be exercised.

Keeping your body as straight as possible, raise your leg to a horizontal position. You should bend the supporting leg slightly.

tion when doing donkey kicks, this creates a shearing force on the disks between the vertebrae of the spine.

HIP EXTENSION
(for a Firmer Backside)

To firm and shape the buttocks, you need to work your gluteus max-imus muscle in a way that puts it up against more resistance than just thin air. You can do Hip Extensions at your fitness club, if you have access to a pulley machine or multi-hip machine (sometimes called a standing hip machine). Or you can do them at home using just ankle weights and a table.

Inhale and pull the cabled leg down and back until your foot is approximately 12 inches—but no farther—to the rear, as shown. Keep your leg straight, and do not lean forward. Exhale and return to the starting position, then repeat.

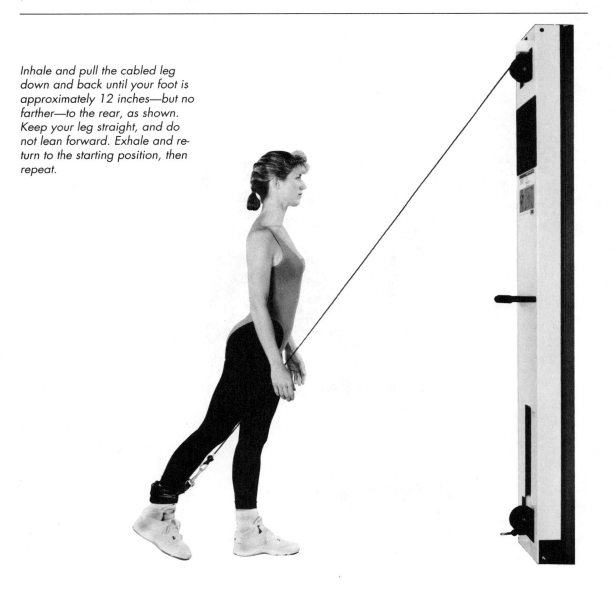

HIP EXTENSION USING A MULTI-HIP MACHINE

Recommended Workloads

Level 1: One set of 3 to 5 repetitions per leg, to start
Level 2: One set of 15 to 20 repetitions per leg
Level 3: Set 1—10 repetitions per leg with half the amount of resistance used in set 2
      Set 2—10 to 12 repetitions per leg maximum
      Set 3—20 repetitions per leg maximum

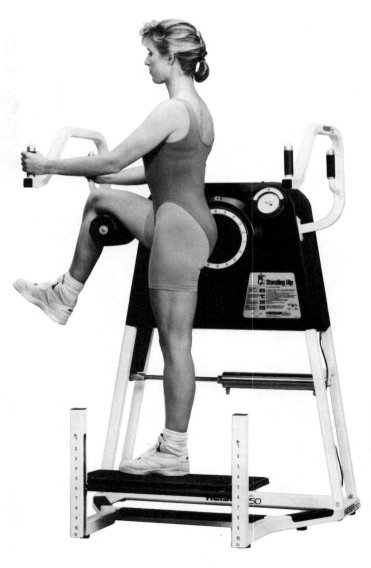

Stand erect with the thigh of one leg resting horizontally on the machine's resistance pad.

To do this exercise using a pulley machine (shown on page 134), it's important to use the high pulley, not the low one. Using the low pulley exercises primarily the muscles of the lower back, not the backside. To give the buttock muscles maximum attention, you need to pull your leg down from a position that's *horizontal* to the ground, as shown. Follow the directions carefully—otherwise, you'll be working your thighs, not your hips.

If you have trouble maintaining your balance when doing this exercise, which is likely at first, feel free to brace yourself for support. You're

Inhale slightly and straighten your leg as you push the leg down and approximately 12 inches to the rear, as shown. Exhale as you allow your leg to return to the horizontal position, then repeat.

HIP EXTENSION USING ANKLE WEIGHTS

Recommended Workloads

Level 1: One set of 3 to 5 repetitions per leg, to start
Level 2: One set of 20 repetitions per leg
Level 3: Set 1—10 repetitions per leg with half the amount of weight used in set 2
       Set 2—10 to 12 repetitions per leg maximum
       Set 3—20 repetitions per leg maximum

With both legs weighted, lie facedown on a padded weight bench with one leg straddling the side of the bench, as shown. Your other leg should remain on the bench. Grasp the edge of the bench for support.

Inhale slightly and raise the leg to be exercised a few inches above the horizontal. Exhale as you lower your leg. Pause, and repeat.

trying to firm your buttocks, not bruise them. (Your balance will improve with time.)

Also, as with all the exercises in this book, be sure to follow the breathing instructions: Inhale *before* doing the exercise, and exhale *after* you complete each repetition. Breathing in this way helps stabilize the midsection, keeps the spine in a safe and proper alignment and also can allow you to generate up to 20 percent more power!

If you prefer, you can do Hip Extensions on what's called a multi-hip or standing hip machine. The foot platform should be adjusted so that the resistance lever arm is at a level that lines up with your hips, as shown on page 136.

As with the pulley machine version of this exercise, it's very important to keep your upper body and the leg being exercised straight. Don't lean forward to assist the motion—the exercise will target the hips but will be less effective.

If you don't have access to either a pulley or a multi-hip machine, don't despair. The same basic exercise can be done at home using ankle weights, exercising first one leg and then the other (see the opposite page). Start with 1-pound weights and work your way up to 5-pound weights.

You can also do this exercise with both legs at the same time. Simply weight both legs, let them both hang off the end of a bench (the higher, the

better), and raise and then lower them simultaneously.

HIP ABDUCTION
(for Firming the Hips)

It can be a little tricky to exercise the hip muscles properly, but it's important to do so to get the kind of toning needed to produce truly noticeable results. These muscles come into play to a moderate degree during fitness activities such as jogging, walking and cycling, but not enough to appreciably tone or reshape the hips.

To firm these muscles significantly, you need to do Hip Abductions, which pull the leg away from the body against some appreciable resistance provided by a pulley machine, a hip abductor machine or weights attached to the ankles. Hip Abductions are also good for tightening the muscles at the sides of the waist just above the hips— the site of those much-maligned love handles.

When performing the Hip Abduction exercise with the pulley machine (shown on page 140), keep your body upright at all times. Giving in to the tendency to lean in toward the machine will substantially reduce the effectiveness of the exercise.

You can also shape your hips by working out on a hip abductor machine (see page 141). But a word of caution regarding positioning: In order to protect the hip joints against irritation, be sure to lie flat or at approxi-

(continued on page 145)

HIP ABDUCTION USING A PULLEY MACHINE

Recommended Workloads

Level 1: One set of 4 to 5 repetitions per leg, to start
Level 2: One set of 15 to 20 repetitions per leg
Level 3: Set 1—10 repetitions per leg with half the amount of resistance used in set 2
Set 2—10 to 12 repetitions per leg maximum
Set 3—20 repetitions per leg maximum

Stand perpendicular to the pulley machine with the cable attached to the leg to be exercised, away from the machine, as shown.

Inhale slightly and pull your cabled leg out to the side as far as possible, as shown, keeping your leg straight and your toes pointed straight ahead or slightly inward. Exhale as you return your leg to the starting position, then repeat.

HIP ABDUCTION USING A HIP ABDUCTOR MACHINE

Recommended Workloads

Level 1: One set of 4 to 5 repetitions, to start

Level 2: One set of 15 to 20 repetitions

Level 3: Set 1—10 repetitions with half the amount of resistance used in set 2

Set 2—10 to 12 repetitions maximum

Set 3—20 repetitions maximum

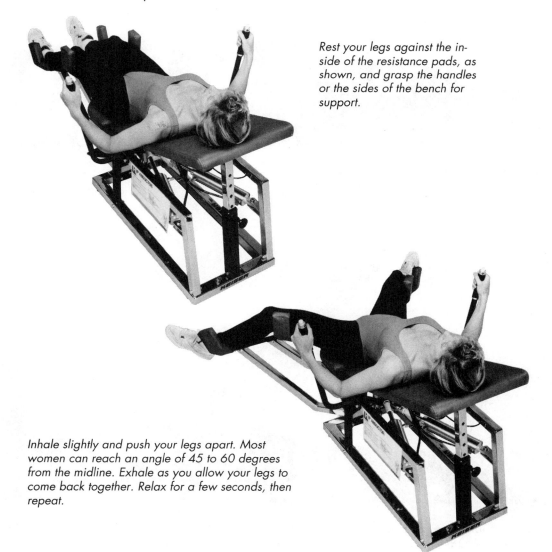

Rest your legs against the inside of the resistance pads, as shown, and grasp the handles or the sides of the bench for support.

Inhale slightly and push your legs apart. Most women can reach an angle of 45 to 60 degrees from the midline. Exhale as you allow your legs to come back together. Relax for a few seconds, then repeat.

Hip Abduction Using Ankle Weights

Recommended Workloads

Level 1: One set of 4 to 5 repetitions per leg, to start

Level 2: One set of 15 to 20 repetitions per leg

Level 3: Set 1—10 repetitions per leg with half the amount of weight used in set 2

     Set 2—10 to 12 repetitions per leg maximum

     Set 3—20 repetitions per leg maximum

Lie on one side with the hips vertical, as shown.

Inhale, then raise your upper leg, as shown. Keep your leg straight and your toes pointed forward. Exhale as you return to the starting position. Repeat.

THE GOOD MORNING

Recommended Workloads

Level 1: One set of 2 to 3 repetitions, to start
Level 2: One set of 10 to 15 repetitions
Level 3: One set of 8 to 10 repetitions plus one set of 20 repetitions

Begin in a standing position (left). Bend forward from the hips, either stopping when your upper body is horizontal to the floor, as shown (right), or as far as your hamstrings will allow. The looser your hamstrings, the farther you can lean. Hold this position for a second or two, then return to the upright position and repeat. Inhale as you bend over and exhale after you are almost vertical.

(continued)

THE GOOD MORNING — CONTINUED

If you can't reach a position horizontal to the floor on your first try, lean forward only as far as feels comfortable, bending your knees if needed (right). As you become more flexible and adept at the maneuver, you can keep your legs progressively straighter. Push your hips to the rear as you bend over.

mately a 30-degree angle *at most,* as shown. If your fitness club has only the type of hip abductor machine that you use in an upright, seated position, be careful not to use it too often—nor to use heavy weights—to avoid injury to the hip joint. Also be sure to keep your toes pointed upward rather than out to the sides.

If you have access to neither a pulley nor a hip abductor machine, you can firm the muscles of the hips nearly as effectively with 1- to 5-pound ankle weights (see page 142).

THE "GOOD MORNING" (for Toning the Buttocks)

So named because it resembles taking a bow, this exercise is yet another highly effective maneuver for toning the muscles of the buttock re-gion, especially the gluteus maximus.

Although the Good Morning (shown on page 143) is an exercise for primarily the buttocks and hamstring muscles, it can also help strengthen the muscles that stabilize the spine, thus helping to improve posture.

To get maximum benefit from the exercise, it's very important to bend from the hips, *not* from the waist. It's also important to keep your back slightly arched (not rounded) and to push your hips to the rear as you lean forward, as shown.

As you become more proficient at this exercise, you can do it while holding dumbbells (1 to 5 pounds) with your arms hanging straight. Later, when you've mastered this, you can pull the dumbbells into your chest, to work the buttock muscles even more.

CHAPTER 12

❖

THE THIGHS
Toning the number one trouble spot

Barbara was lamenting the size of her thighs.

"I can't believe it, Dr. Yessis," she wailed. "My boyfriend is six feet tall and weighs 180 pounds, and I am only five-five and weigh 138. We got the tape measure out the other night, and my thighs are the same size as his! I don't know whether to be more embarrassed or depressed."

Barbara's tale of the tape, as much as it perplexed, did not surprise me. Women tend to carry excess weight in the area of their thighs more so than men for a very practical reason: to provide greater strength and stability for carrying a fetus during pregnancy. From a standpoint of basic survival, large, strong thighs give the female physique a definite advantage. Over the thousands of years that humans have evolved, women who could be the most mobile during their pregnancies were the ones who had the greatest chances of surviving, hence passing on the genetic tendency for large thighs to their offspring.

All of which I explained to Barbara.

"So you're saying that some distant relative of mine had large thighs and that I'm locked in a losing battle with Mother Nature?" Barbara asked.

"Not a losing one, just not an easy one," was my reply. "If you want smaller, firmer and more shapely thighs, you're going to have to work for them. You're going to have to reduce the amount of extra body fat you carry, but you also have to tone and tighten the muscles of your thighs in particular."

I wished I could've told Barbara there is an easier way, but there isn't.

"What about body wrapping?" she asked. She'd read somewhere about a technique touted as a quick way to get rid of cellulite and other unwanted pounds in the thigh area.

"Sure, you could have your thighs wrapped and squeezed in cellophane for a pretty penny," I said. "But I can guarantee you that the only thing you'd be losing is your money. The results of body wrapping are barely noticeable and very short-lived."

What about liposuction?

"Removing fat from the thighs—

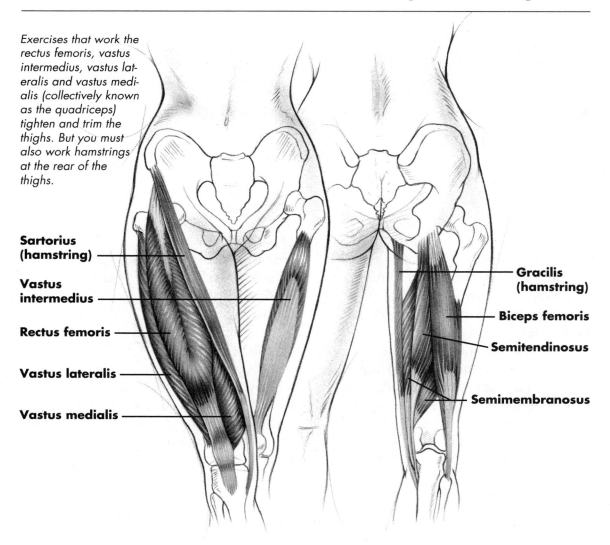

Exercises that work the rectus femoris, vastus intermedius, vastus lateralis and vastus medialis (collectively known as the quadriceps) tighten and trim the thighs. But you must also work hamstrings at the rear of the thighs.

Sartorius (hamstring)

Vastus intermedius

Rectus femoris

Vastus lateralis

Vastus medialis

Gracilis (hamstring)

Biceps femoris

Semitendinosus

Semimembranosus

yes, it works," I told her. "But it's also prohibitively expensive, and it does nothing to alter your lifestyle in ways to prevent the fat from returning. (To say nothing of the risk of complications.) Yet I've known women to undergo the procedure far more often than they'd care to admit."

Surprisingly, Barbara was not discouraged by my honesty. She was rather inspired, in fact. "My boyfriend has been hounding me about getting in better shape anyway, because he works out," she said. "I guess we'll just start working out together."

A PERMANENT SOLUTION TO HEAVY THIGHS

One year later, Barbara's tape told a different tale. She lost two inches off her thighs, while her boyfriend put on an inch and a half—"All muscle, though," Barbara was quick to report. "He has been working out as hard as I have and looks really great."

But enough inspiration; time for some perspiration. Let's look at the exercises that can trim and firm the thighs best.

Because the muscles at the front and back of the thigh line up vertically and form a cylindrical column, they may look like one long muscle. But the thigh is actually several muscles, plus connecting tendons. It consists of four muscles at the front of the thigh (collectively known as the quadriceps) plus several muscles collectively known as the hamstrings. (See the illustration on page 147.)

What this means is that optimal shaping and toning of the thighs takes more than just a single aerobic exercise such as jogging or rope jumping, which is the approach many women take to slimming and firming this troublesome area. This isn't to say that these activities are a waste—they are very effective cardiovascular fitness builders and great calorie burners and help trim away body fat overall. But to give the thighs maximal firmness and shape, you must work the individual thigh muscles. This individual attention, combined with a regular fat- and calorie-burning activity such as running, walking, cycling, swimming or rope jumping, is the best way to trim and tighten the thigh area.

That said, let's look at the exercises that best target the thigh muscles.

LEG EXTENSION
(for the Mid- to Lower Portion of the Muscles of the Front of the Thighs)

You can do this exercise with either a leg extension machine (shown on the opposite page) or ankle weights.

If you use a leg extension machine, be sure to adjust the seat height and back support so that you can place the insteps of your feet and the base of your shins against the inner side of the padded resistance bar or rollers. You may also find it's more comfortable to lean back at approximately a 20- to 30-

LEG EXTENSION USING A LEG EXTENSION MACHINE

Recommended Workloads

Level 1: One set of 3 to 4 repetitions, to start
Level 2: One set of 15 to 20 repetitions
Level 3: Set 1—10 repetitions with half the amount of resistance used in set 2
Set 2—10 to 12 repetitions maximum
Set 3—20 repetitions maximum

Sit on the leg extension machine so that the back of your knees doesn't quite hit the edge of the bench and your lower legs hang vertically at a 90-degree angle, as shown. Hold on to the grips alongside the bench for support. To minimize stress on the knees, don't allow your legs to bend back—that is, with your calves under your thighs.

Inhale slightly and push the resistance bar forward and upward until your legs are straight and your knees are locked. Exhale as you allow your legs to return to the starting position. Repeat.

LEG EXTENSION USING ANKLE WEIGHTS

Recommended Workloads

Level 1: One set of 3 to 4 repetitions per leg, to start

Level 2: One set of 15 to 20 repetitions per leg

Level 3: Set 1—10 repetitions per leg with half the amount of weight used in set 2

Set 2—10 to 12 repetitions per leg maximum

Set 3—20 repetitions per leg maximum

Sit on a padded weight bench as shown. Grasp the sides of the bench for support.

Inhale slightly and raise your leg until it's straight and your knee is locked. Exhale as you lower your leg to the starting position. Repeat with opposite leg.

If you prefer, you can raise both legs simultaneously.

degree angle from vertical, as shown.

Variations: To concentrate more on the inner thigh, turn your toes outward as you raise the resistance bar and on the return. To direct the exercise more to the outer part of the thigh, turn your toes inward as you raise the bar about halfway up and turn them

---

LEG CURL USING A LEG CURL MACHINE

Recommended Workloads

Level 1: One set of 3 to 4 repetitions, to start
Level 2: One set of 10 to 15 repetitions
Level 3: Set 1—10 repetitions with half the amount of resistance used in set 2
Set 2—10 to 12 repetitions maximum
Set 3—20 repetitions maximum

Sit on the leg curl machine with your thighs in full contact with the seat (spine against the backrest, knees at the front of the seat) and your lower calves resting against the resistance pad. For support, grasp the handles on the retaining bar, as shown here (or on the sides of the bench on other machines), and move the retaining bar into place to stabilize your thighs.

(continued)

straight as you lower the bar.

To perform this exercise using ankle weights, you should begin with 2 to 5 pounds per ankle. You can sit up straight if you prefer, or you can lean back, which is better (see page 150).

LEG CURL
(for the Mid- to Lower Portion of the Back of the Thighs)

It's as important to strengthen the muscles in the rear of the thighs as it is those in the front, partly for appearance' sake and partly to prevent dis-

---

LEG CURL USING A LEG CURL MACHINE—CONTINUED

Inhale and bend your knees, stopping when your lower legs are slightly past the vertical, as shown. Exhale as you allow your legs to return to the starting position. Repeat.

LEG CURL USING ANKLE WEIGHTS

Recommended Workloads

Level 1: One set of 3 to 4 repetitions, to start
Level 2: One set of 10 to 15 repetitions
Level 3: Set 1—10 repetitions with half the amount of weight used in set 2
 Set 2—10 to 20 repetitions maximum
 Set 3—20 to 25 repetitions maximum

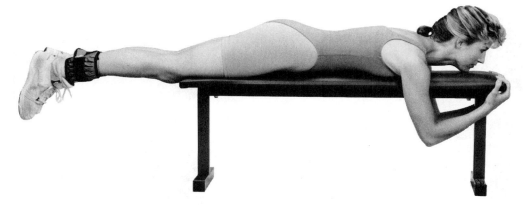

Lie facedown on a padded weight bench. Grasp the edge of the bench for support.

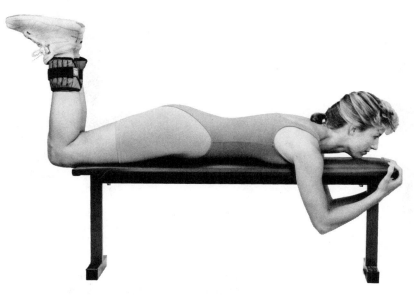

*Inhale and bend your knees, stopping when your lower legs have reached a position
slightly past the vertical.*

(continued)

proportionate muscle development: If the quads are strong but the hamstrings are weak, you risk an injury. Also, the stronger your hamstrings, the stronger your quads become. So if you're doing Leg Extensions, you should also do Leg Curls—they strengthen and firm the hamstrings.

And as with the Leg Extensions, you can do Leg Curls either on a leg

---

LEG CURL USING ANKLE WEIGHTS—CONTINUED

If you prefer, you can perform this exercise while standing. (Hold on to a wall for support.) Stand with your feet about six inches apart.

Inhale and raise the leg being exercised until your shin is approximately horizontal to the floor, as shown, or slightly above. Exhale as you lower your leg to the floor. Repeat.

curl machine or with ankle weights, either standing or lying on an angled weight bench. A leg curl machine is preferable—it works the muscles more effectively and eliminates the possibility that you will arch the back (see page 151). (If an angled bench is not available, a flat one will do: Simply place a small, rolled-up towel under your lower abdomen.)

If you don't have access to a leg curl machine, you can do this same exercise using ankle weights (as shown on page 153). Use 2 to 5 pounds of weight per leg.

LEG ADDUCTION
(for the Muscles of the Inner Thighs)

The muscles of the inner thigh are odd in that they are among the largest of the body yet they perform a very limited function: They help pull the legs inward from a spread position, and that's essentially it. Unless you happen to ride bulls in a rodeo, you probably don't get a great deal of use out of these muscles—at least none that you notice.

Limited use is perhaps why these muscles become soft and out of shape. But we can fix that: The pulling action exerted in this exercise will give your inner thighs a good workout. You can use a hip adductor machine, a low pulley apparatus or ankle weights.

If you use a hip adductor machine (shown on page 156), adjust the resistance pads so that you can spread your legs as far apart as is comfortably possible. Doing this exercise with your legs spread too wide when you first start out could injure the muscles you're trying to tone. You may, however, increase the distance between the resistance pads later, as you develop greater flexibility and proficiency with the exercise.

The instructions are for a machine made by Keiser, but you can follow the same principles on other makes.

To perform this exact same exercise on a pulley machine, follow the instructions on page 158. Be sure to stand erect and hold on to the pulley machine for support. If you cheat and lean to one side, you lose the benefits.

Ankle weights are not the most effective way to work the inner thigh, but they'll do if you don't have access to a hip adductor or pulley machine. Use 1 to 2 pounds of weight on each leg (see page 159).

LEG ABDUCTION
(for the Outside of the Thighs)

The outer thigh muscles' main function is to pull the leg out to the side and to keep the pelvis level as you walk or run. As with the inner thigh muscles, you can work these muscles on a weight machine (abductor), with a pulley apparatus or using ankle weights.

Set the hip abductor machine's resistance to the level that you desire.

LEG ADDUCTION USING A HIP ADDUCTOR MACHINE

Recommended Workloads

Level 1: One set of 3 to 4 repetitions, to start
Level 2: One set of 10 to 15 repetitions
Level 3: Set 1—10 repetitions with half the amount of resistance used in set 2
Set 2—10 to 15 repetitions maximum
Set 3—15 to 25 repetitions maximum

Lie on your back so that your pelvis is on the seat of the machine and the inside of your lower thighs and upper ankles are in contact with the resistance pads, as shown.

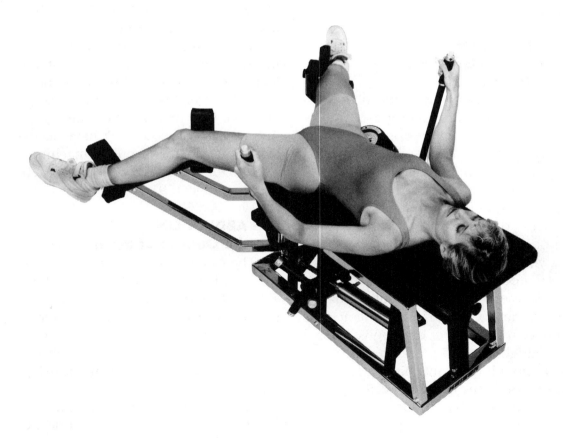

Again, the instructions on page 160 are specific to a machine made by Keiser, though they can be adapted to most other hip abductor machines with little difficulty.

To work the outer thighs using a low pulley apparatus, follow the instructions on page 162. Stand as erect as possible—this exercise will not be as effective if you give in to the tendency to lean in toward the machine.

To work the outer thighs using ankle weights instead of weight

(continued on page 160)

Inhale and push your legs together until the thigh pads meet. Exhale as you slowly allow your legs to return to the starting position. Repeat.

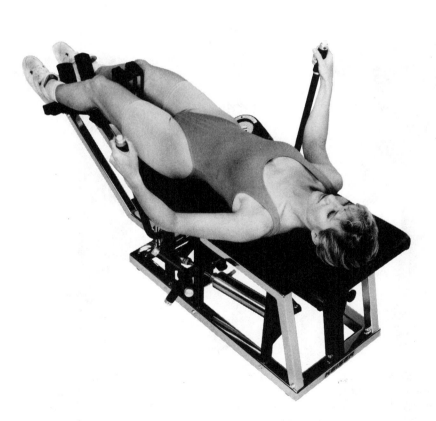

LEG ADDUCTION USING A LOW PULLEY MACHINE

Recommended Workloads

Level 1: One set of 3 to 4 repetitions per leg, to start
Level 2: One set of 10 to 15 repetitions per leg
Level 3: Set 1—10 repetitions per leg with half the amount of resistance used in set 2
Set 2—10 to15 repetitions per leg maximum
Set 3—15 to 25 repetitions per leg maximum

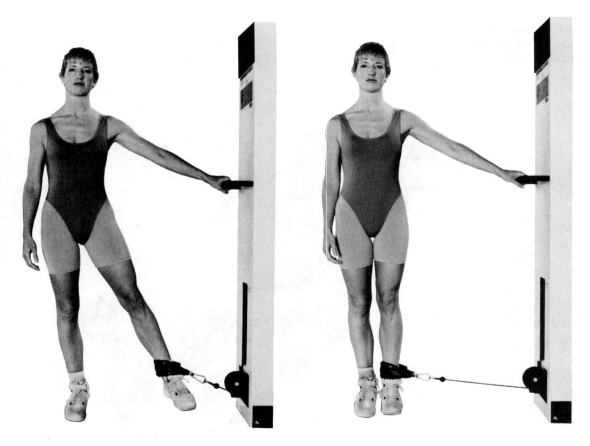

Attach the pulley cable to the leg closest to the pulley and stand perpendicular to the machine, with your feet slightly more than shoulder-width apart. Shift your weight onto your outside leg.

Then inhale slightly and pull the cable inward until the exercised leg meets the other leg. Relax, then repeat.

LEG ADDUCTION USING ANKLE WEIGHTS

Recommended Workloads

Level 1: One set of 3 to 4 repetitions per leg, to start

Level 2: One set of 10 to 15 repetitions per leg

Level 3: Set 1—10 repetitions per leg with half the amount of weight used in set 2

Set 2—10 to 15 repetitions per leg maximum

Set 3—20 to 25 repetitions per leg maximum

Lie on your side with your top leg forward as shown.

Inhale slightly and raise your lower leg as high as you comfortably can. Exhale as you then lower the leg. Repeat.

machines, follow the instructions on page 163, using 2 to 5 pounds of weight on each ankle. Be sure to keep your toes pointed straight ahead or slightly downward. Turning your foot so that your toes are pointing up will defeat the purpose of the exercise.

THE SQUAT
(for Both the Front and Rear of the Thighs plus the Buttocks)

The Squat has long been considered the king of all exercises, and for good reason: It works not just both the front and rear of the thigh muscles but

---

LEG ABDUCTION USING A HIP ABDUCTOR MACHINE

Recommended Workloads

Level 1: One set of 3 to 4 repetitions, to start
Level 2: One set of 10 repetitions
Level 3: Set 1—10 repetitions with half the amount of resistance used in set 2
     Set 2—10 repetitions maximum
     Set 3—15 to 20 repetitions maximum

Lower the back support so that you're lying flat, with your pelvis directly over the seat and the resistance pads slightly above your knees and ankles, as shown. Your hands should be grasping the machine's handles for support.

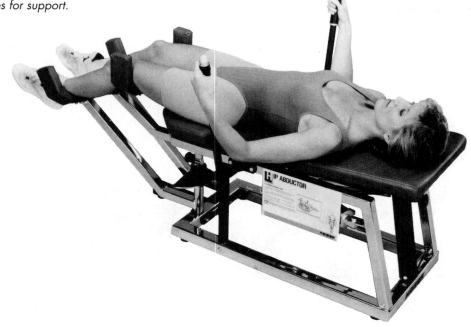

the knees, buttocks and, to a limited degree, lower back as well. It's important not to be too ambitious when doing Squats, however, as injury can result. Proper technique is paramount, as is choosing the proper weight. If you're brand-new to the exercise, in fact, you should use no added weight—after all, you will be raising your body weight.

If you aren't flexible enough to reach the position shown in the photos, just do the best you can. It's also

(continued on page 164)

Inhale and spread your legs as far apart as is comfortably possible. Exhale as you bring your legs back together. Repeat.

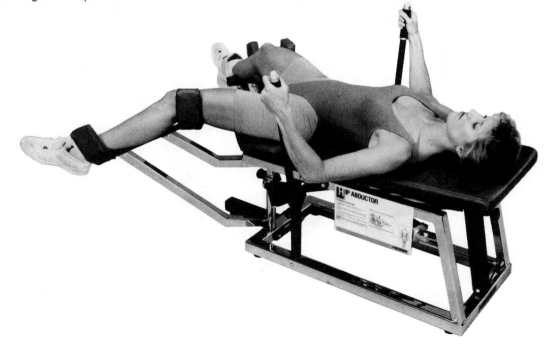

Leg Abduction Using a Low Pulley Machine

Recommended Workloads

Level 1: One set of 3 to 4 repetitions per leg, to start

Level 2: One set of 10 repetitions per leg

Level 3: Set 1—8 repetitions per leg with half the amount of resistance used in set 2

Set 2—10 repetitions per leg maximum

Set 3—15 to 20 repetitions per leg maximum

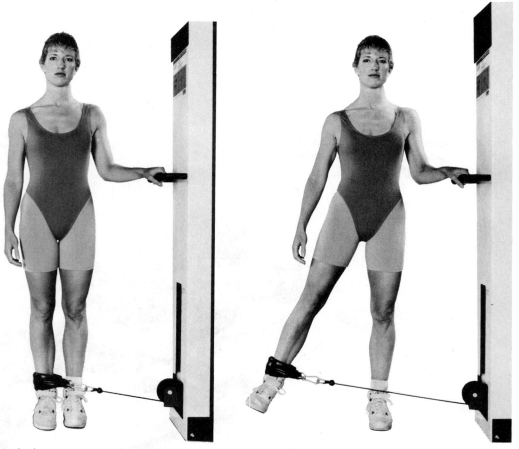

Stand alongside the apparatus with your feet together, your toes pointed forward and the cable attached to the leg farthest from the machine.

Inhale slightly and pull your cabled leg as far away from your other leg as possible. Keep your leg and your foot straight (or your leg straight and your foot turned slightly inward). Exhale as you allow your cabled leg to return to the starting position. Repeat.

LEG ABDUCTION USING ANKLE WEIGHTS

Recommended Workloads

Level 1: One set of 3 to 4 repetitions per leg, to start

Level 2: One set of 10 to 15 repetitions per leg

Level 3: Set 1—5 to 8 repetitions per leg with half the amount of weight used in set 2

Set 2—10 repetitions per leg maximum

Set 3—15 to 20 repetitions per leg maximum

Lie on your side with the leg to be exercised facing up. Your body should be in a straight line, and one arm should be outstretched while the other is at your side as shown.

Inhale slightly and raise the leg being exercised as high as possible, keeping it straight, as shown. Exhale as you lower that leg. Relax, then repeat.

important to keep your eyes focused straight ahead to help you maintain your balance.

Incidentally, the Good Morning exercise for the hips, described in chapter 11, is a good way to warm up before doing Squats.

We'll look at the unweighted ver-

UNWEIGHTED SQUAT

Recommended Workloads

Level 1: One set of 3 to 4 repetitions, to start
Level 2: One set of 10 to 15 repetitions
Level 3: One set of 10 repetitions plus one set of 15 to 20 repetitions

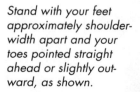

Stand with your feet approximately shoulder-width apart and your toes pointed straight ahead or slightly outward, as shown.

Inhale and lower yourself into the squat position, stopping when your thighs have reached a position parallel to the floor, as shown. At this point, your arms should be extended straight ahead, your back should be slightly arched, and your heels should remain in contact with the floor in order to avoid undue stress on your knees.

sion first; see the instructions on the opposite page. Once you feel comfortable doing Squats in the unweighted manner, you can begin adding some resistance to increase the benefits of the exercise. This can be done by using a single barbell, dumbbells or what's known as a squat machine.

To perform Squats using a barbell, follow the instructions on page 166; if you're using dumbbells, follow the instructions on page 168.

To perform Squats using a squat machine, follow the directions on page 170. If using a Keiser machine, as

(continued on page 173)

Begin to raise yourself back up, exhaling after you pass the most difficult point of your return trip. Do not exhale completely until you are once again fully standing. (Breathing in this manner is important for helping you maintain the arch in your lower back and hence preventing undue strain on the muscles of the lower portion of the spine.)

Inhale again and repeat.

Squat Using a Barbell

Recommended Workloads

Level 1: One set of 3 to 4 repetitions without additional weight, to start
Level 2: One set of 10 to 15 repetitions with 10 to 20 pounds total weight
Level 3: Set 1—10 repetitions without additional weight
       Set 2—10 to 15 repetitions maximum with 30 to 40 pounds total weight
       Set 3—20 repetitions maximum with 20 pounds total weight

Stand with your feet about shoulder-width apart and your toes pointed straight ahead. Hold a barbell behind your neck, across your shoulders, as shown. Your grip should be a little wider than shoulder-width, but you can vary this to whatever is comfortable for you.

Inhale, bend your knees, and slowly lower your body. Your buttocks should move to the rear, and your trunk should move forward slightly. Keep your spine arched, your thighs horizontal (or close to it) and your heels on the floor.

Reverse direction
by straightening
your legs. Begin
to exhale just
after you reach
the most difficult
part of the move.

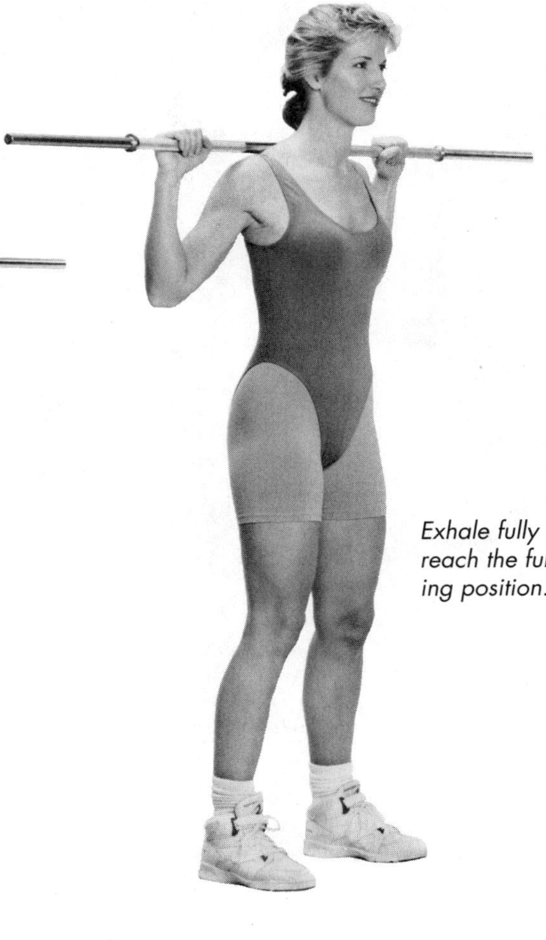

Exhale fully as you
reach the full stand-
ing position.

SQUAT USING DUMBBELLS

Recommended Workloads

Level 1: One set of 3 to 4 repetitions without weight, to start
Level 2: One set of 15 to 20 repetitions with 5- to 8-pound dumbbells
Level 3: Set 1—10 repetitions without weight
            Set 2—10 repetitions maximum with 5- to 10-pound dumbbells
            Set 3—20 repetitions maximum with 5-pound dumbbells

Stand with your feet shoulder-width apart, holding the dumbbells alongside your body. Inhale and raise the dumbbells to your shoulders, then exhale. (This is the starting position.) Inhale and lower your body until your thighs are parallel to the floor. Pause for a second or two, then rise to the starting position. Exhale and repeat.

Alternate: Stand with your feet shoulder-width apart, holding the dumbbells facing forward. Inhale and raise the dumbbells to your shoulders, then exhale. (This is the starting position.) Inhale and lower your body until your thighs are parallel to the floor. Pause for a second or two, then rise to the starting position. Exhale and repeat.

SQUAT USING A SQUAT MACHINE

Recommended Workloads

Level 1: One set of 3 to 5 repetitions without additional resistance, to start

Level 2: One set of 15 to 20 repetitions without additional resistance or with 10 to 15 pounds additional resistance

Level 3: Set 1—10 repetitions without additional resistance
Set 2—10 repetitions maximum with 20 pounds additional resistance
Set 3—20 repetitions maximum with 10 to 15 pounds additional resistance

To begin, lower yourself into a semi-squat position with your feet about 10 to 12 inches in front of your shoulders, as shown, and grasp the handles (or the shoulder resistance pads, if your machine has no handles).

Pushing against the resistance pads and keeping your spine vertical, raise yourself into an upright position.

Inhale and lower your body until your thighs are parallel to the floor and there is a 90-degree angle between your trunk and thighs and your thighs and shins. Raise, and after passing the most difficult part of the lift, exhale. Pause and repeat.

LUNGE USING A BARBELL

Recommended Workloads

Level 1: One set of 2 to 3 repetitions per leg without additional weight

Level 2: One set of 15 to 20 repetitions per leg without additional weight

Level 3: Set 1—5 to 8 repetitions per leg without additional weight

Set 2—10 repetitions per leg maximum with 20 pounds additional weight

Set 3—15 to 20 repetitions per leg maximum with 10 pounds additional weight

Stand in a well-balanced position with your feet slightly more than hip-width apart, as shown.

Inhale and step forward with as long a stride as possible, keeping your trunk erect and your back slightly arched, as shown.

Now lower yourself until your hip muscles begin to feel taut. (When you've developed good flexibility in doing this exercise, you should be able to reach a position where the knee of your rear leg lightly touches the floor, in a relaxed but straight position.)

shown in the photos, adjust the resistance using the resistance buttons on the frame.

LUNGE
(for Quads, Hamstrings, Hips and Buttocks)

Yet another staple exercise, the Lunge works both the front and rear of the thighs plus the hips and buttocks all in one fell swoop. It's impor-tant when doing Lunges, however, to do just that: *lunge.* The longer the stride you can take, the more effective the exercise.

You can do Lunges with or without a barbell held at your chest (or two dumbbells held at your sides) for added weight (see the opposite page). But I recommend not using any weight until you familiarize yourself with the exercise.

Shift your weight backward and take as many small steps as needed with your forward leg (left) to return to a standing position (right). Exhale, pause, and repeat with other leg.

LEG PRESS
(for the Thighs)

The Leg Press is excellent for working the quadriceps (front of the thighs) and upper hamstrings (rear of the thighs). Unlike Squats and Lunges, performing Leg Presses does not require careful balance. Be sure not to bring the knees too close to the chest. Doing so rounds the lower back and can cause injury.

If you use a Keiser machine, as shown below, adjust the resistance after getting into position. If you use a machine with weight plates, set the amount before you begin.

LEG PRESS USING A LEG PRESS MACHINE

Recommended Workloads

Level 1: One set of 2 to 3 repetitions without additional resistance

Level 2: One set of 15 to 20 repetitions with 10 pounds additional resistance

Level 3: Set 1—10 repetitions without additional resistance

Set 2—10 repetitions maximum with 20 to 30 pounds additional resistance

Set 3—15 to 20 repetitions maximum with 10 to 15 pounds additional resistance

Sit on the leg press machine with your feet resting fully against the resistance plate. Lean against the backrest with your hips flush against the back support.

Inhale and push forward until your legs are straight but not locked. (This is the start position.) Exhale and relax somewhat.

Inhale and bend your knees at a 90-degree angle, as shown, then extend again. Exhale, pause, then repeat.

CHAPTER 13

❖

THE CALVES AND ANKLES
The quest for lovelier legs

ook for yourself," Katherine said as she hiked her sweatpants above her knees. "My calves and ankles are about as shapeless as the legs of our dining room table."

I'd never seen Katherine's dining room table. But from what I saw, she was probably right. Katherine's ankles were relatively thick, and her calves were not very well developed or defined. Together, Katherine's calves and ankles were "reminiscent of Olive Oyl" (Katherine's assessment, not mine). Were shapeless calves and ankles something Katherine would "just have to learn to live with," she wanted to know.

Before I could give Katherine an honest answer, I needed to take a closer look. No, there wasn't a lot of fat responsible for the thickness of her ankles, so a general weight loss program wasn't going to have much effect there.

Sometimes, ankles can swell due to water retention (edema), which is a possible result of a heart condition or another circulatory problem or of an excess of sodium in the diet. This possibility should always be checked out with a doctor, who may suggest that you reduce the sodium in your diet for several weeks to see if you notice a difference. Given the unhealthful effects excess sodium is known to have on some people's blood pressure, you certainly have nothing to lose—except maybe some ankle girth—by investi-

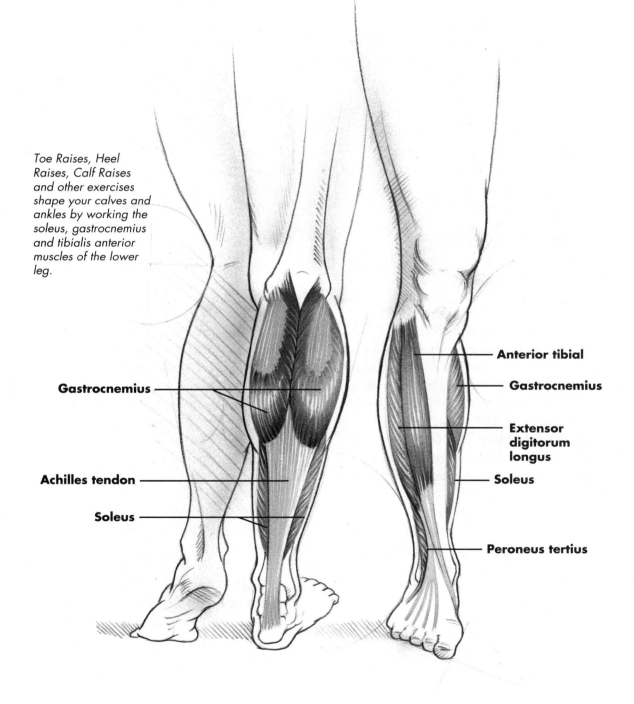

Toe Raises, Heel Raises, Calf Raises and other exercises shape your calves and ankles by working the soleus, gastrocnemius and tibialis anterior muscles of the lower leg.

Gastrocnemius

Achilles tendon

Soleus

Anterior tibial

Gastrocnemius

Extensor digitorum longus

Soleus

Peroneus tertius

gating this connection.

Katherine had checked with her doctor, though, and water retention wasn't a problem. As I suspected, Katherine's calf muscles were simply underdeveloped. So there *was* room for improvement after all.

"What we're going to have to do is a little camouflaging," I told her. "You're not carrying a lot of body fat generally, so losing weight isn't the answer—it wouldn't reduce the size of your ankles by very much. But there are very specific muscle-toning exercises that can enhance the size and shape of your calf muscles, thus making your ankles appear thinner by comparison."

ANATOMY OF AN ANKLE

Katherine was encouraged. But she also had a good question. If she wasn't overweight, and she wasn't retaining water, *why* were her ankles thick?

"Three words," I said. "Bone, tendon and genes. In the absence of excess body fat or water retention, thicker-than-average ankles are the combined result of thick ankle bones and a thick Achilles tendon, which runs up to the back of the calf muscle from the heel. You inherit these physiological quirks, and there's not much you can do to change bone or tendons.

"What you *can* change, however, is the size and shape of your calf muscles, so this is where our attention will go," I went on to explain.

The upper calf is comprised essentially of two muscles—the gastrocnemius and the soleus. Running, rope jumping and stair climbing also are good exercises for these muscles and tendons. Sustained activities like these build endurance and firm the muscles to some degree, but not the way highly focused, muscle-building exercises (such as the Heel Raise) can. To increase the calves and give them a rounder and fuller shape, the Heel Raise is the answer.

"With the right exercises, you'll be able to build and shape your calves so that your ankles will 'shrink' in appearance, if not actual size," I told Katherine.

One year after this crash course in ankle physiology, Katherine was no longer wearing floor-length skirts to hide what she had feared was a genetic fate. She had built up her calves, giving them firmness and form, the result being not just shapelier legs but much stronger ones. "I'm on my feet all day in my job, and I don't feel nearly as wiped out at the end of the day as I used to," she told me.

Let's look at the exercises that helped Katherine's little anatomical "miracle" come true.

HEEL RAISE
(for Rounder and Firmer Calves)

No exercise develops the upper calf muscles, giving the area a few inches below the knee a firmer, rounder appearance, better than the

HEEL RAISE USING A HEEL RAISE MACHINE

Recommended Workloads

Level 1: One set of 3 to 4 repetitions, to start

Level 2: One set of 15 to 20 repetitions

Level 3: Set 1—10 repetitions without additional resistance or with 10 pounds additional resistance

Set 2—10 to15 repetitions maximum with 40 to 50 pounds additional resistance

Set 3—20 repetitions maximum with 20 to 30 pounds additional resistance

Starting position: Stand with the balls of your feet on the platform of the heel raise machine. Squat slightly, keeping your back slightly arched, to position your shoulders beneath the resistance pads. Press your shoulders against the pads, straightening your legs and trunk. You are now ready to begin.

(continued)

Heel Raise. As we saw with Katherine, this can be an effective way to minimize the appearance, if not the actual size, of large ankles.

You can do Heel Raises on a heel raise machine found in most health clubs (see page 179). Or you can do them on just about any raised surface,

---

HEEL RAISE USING A HEEL RAISE MACHINE — CONTINUED

Inhale slightly, then lower your heels until you feel a slight stretch in both your calf muscles and Achilles tendons, as shown. Go as low as you can without excessive strain, because the greater the range of motion you can achieve, the greater the effects of the exercise.

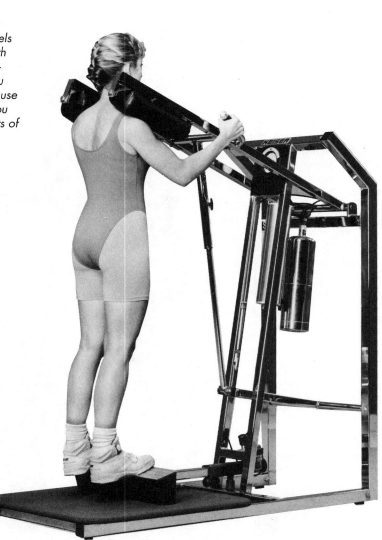

such as an exercise step (as shown on page 182) or a stair (as shown on page 184). You'll need fairly good balance for this, and it could be a little tricky at first. But you should get better with practice. To get maximum results from Heel Raises, it's important to go through as wide a range of motion as

When you've reached this lower-most point, raise your heels as high as you can, keeping your back and legs straight. Hold this position for a second or two, then exhale as you return to the starting position, and repeat.

HEEL RAISE USING AN EXERCISE STEP AND WEIGHTS

Recommended Workloads

Level 1: One set of 3 to 4 repetitions, to start
Level 2: One set of 15 to 20 repetitions
Level 3: Set 1—10 repetitions without weight
　　　　　 Set 2—15 repetitions maximum with weight
　　　　　 Set 3—20 to 25 repetitions maximum with weight

Starting position: Stand on the edge of an exercise step (shown here) or any stable raised surface that's high enough to keep your heels from coming in contact with the floor. Hold a light (10- to 15-pound) barbell across your shoulders (left) or a 5- to 8-pound dumbbell at each side (center).

possible (that is, raising as high on your toes and lowering your heels as far as you comfortably can) while keeping your legs straight.

Variation: To work the calf mus-

cles as fully as possible, do some Heel Raises with your toes pointed slightly inward and some with your toes pointed slightly outward.

(continued on page 186)

Inhale slightly, then lower yourself as much as you can without tottering backward (above left and on the opposite page at right), until you feel a slight stretch in both your calf muscles and Achilles tendons (the same as in the machine version of this exercise). Raise your heels as high as you can, as shown (center and right), keeping your back and legs straight. Hold this position for a second or two, then exhale as you return to the starting position, and repeat.

HEEL RAISE USING A STAIR RISER

Recommended Workloads

Level 1: One set of 3 to 4 repetitions, to start
Level 2: One set of 15 to 20 repetitions
Level 3: One set of 12 repetitions plus one set of 20 repetitions

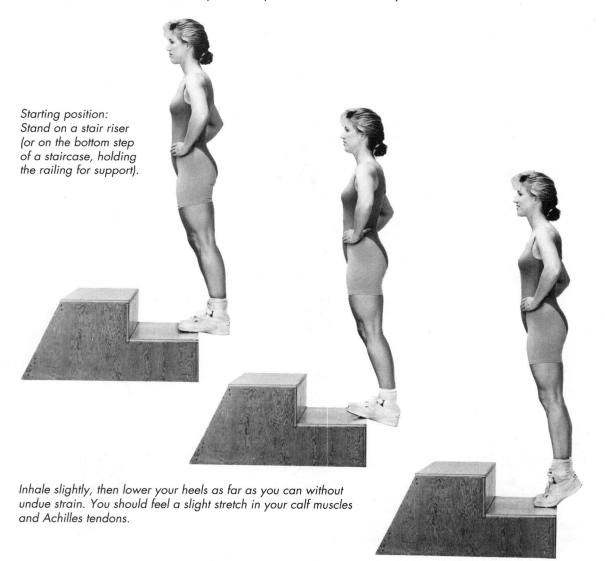

*Starting position:
Stand on a stair riser
(or on the bottom step
of a staircase, holding
the railing for support).*

*Inhale slightly, then lower your heels as far as you can without
undue strain. You should feel a slight stretch in your calf muscles
and Achilles tendons.*

*Raise your heels as high as you can, keeping your back and legs straight.
Hold for a second or two, then exhale and return to the starting position.*

SEATED CALF RAISE USING A MACHINE

Recommended Workloads

Level 1: One set of 3 to 4 repetitions, to start
Level 2: One set of 15 to 20 repetitions
Level 3: Set 1—5 to 8 repetitions with half the amount of resistance used in set 2
         Set 2—10 to 12 repetitions maximum
         Set 3—20 repetitions maximum

Sit on the weight machine with the balls of your feet firmly pressed against the angled foot platform. Grasp the handles of the machine and pull the padded resistance bar over your lower thighs.

Once in position, set the resistance to the level you desire, inhale slightly, and raise your heels as high as possible, as shown. For maximum effect, hold this position for a second or two, then exhale as you lower your heels to the starting position. Inhale again, and repeat.

SEATED CALF RAISE
(for Fuller Calves)

While the gastrocnemius muscle is responsible for fullness at the rear of the calf, the soleus muscle is respon- sible for fullness at the sides of the calf. So it will take more than just Heel Raises to achieve a truly "well-rounded" calf. The Seated Calf Raise targets the soleus muscle (although the

---

SEATED CALF RAISE USING A BARBELL

Recommended Workloads

Level 1: One set of 3 to 4 repetitions, to start
Level 2: One set of 10 to 15 repetitions
Level 3: Set 1—5 to 8 repetitions with half the amount of weight used in set 2
Set 2—10 to 12 repetitions maximum
Set 3—20 repetitions maximum

Sit on a bench or chair with a weighted barbell across your knees. Rest the balls of your feet on a block or another raised surface. Your heels should not touch the floor when your feet are fully flexed.

Inhale slightly, then raise your heels as high as you can. For maximum effect, hold this position for a second or two.

Exhale as you lower your heels as far as possible without touching the floor. Return to the starting position.

Heel Raise also works this muscle to some degree).

If you don't have access to a weight machine for this exercise (see page 185), you can do nearly as well sitting on a padded weight bench, with a weighted barbell across your knees (to provide the resistance otherwise

---

TOE RAISES USING ANKLE WEIGHTS

Recommended Workloads

Level 1: One set of 3 to 5 repetitions, to start
Level 2: One set of 15 to 20 repetitions
Level 3: Set 1—8 repetitions with half the amount of weight used in set 2
           Set 2—10 to 15 repetitions maximum
           Set 3—25 repetitions maximum

Sit on a padded weight bench with your lower legs hanging free, as shown. Flexing your ankles, raise your toes as high as possible.

provided by the machine) and an exercise step, a block or another stable surface about two to four inches high (to raise your feet off the floor), as shown on page 186. (The calf muscles are very powerful, so for this exercise you can use 20 to 40 pounds of weight.)

TOE RAISE
(to Further Shape the Lower Leg)

The muscles of the lower legs, alongside and in front of the shinbone, have names that sound like Roman emperors—peroneus tertius, extensor digitorum longus, tibialis anterior and so forth.

Lower your toes as far as possible, then repeat.

Exercising can build up the muscles over the upper shin and "correct" bony, piano-leg shins. As a bonus, resistance exercises for the lower legs can also prevent shin splints, for which you'll be grateful if you rely on running regularly to burn fat and calories. But few normal, everyday activities work these muscles. Enter the Toe Raise.

Toe Raises are quite simple: All you need is a 1- to 2-pound ankle weight strapped to the ball of each foot, as shown on page 188. You'll need added height, so this is best done on an adjustable weight bench. Some people prop up one end of the bench with a weight plate.

If you progress to the point where ankle weights no longer seem to provide substantial resistance, you can use a weight shoe for additional resistance.

❖

CHAPTER 14

THE BODY SHAPING DIET PLAN

Eat better, not less

Now for the fun part. That's right, the fun part. If you've been wondering what dietary efforts your Body Shaping will require, I think you'll be pleasantly surprised. The well-shaped body is not a deprived body. It's a well-nourished, energetic and satisfied body.

Don't get me wrong: This isn't to say you're going to be able to build your "temple" out of Twinkies. But it does mean you shouldn't be trying to shape up by living on clear broths or thin air, either. "Dieting" in the traditional sense removes fat from every part of your body. You might take inches off your hips, but your breasts will shrink, too. You'll just be a smaller, skinnier version of the old

you. Traditional, rigid diets are the antithesis of what I'm going to describe here.

If you are tired of the way you look and want to make substantial changes in your physique, you're going to have to give your body the right "fuels" to do it. Hunger pangs, headaches, bizarre supplements, cravings, fasts and/or binges aren't part of the Body Shaping plan.

So often I see women try to go on austere "diets" when they begin to exercise, only to end up grumpy, tired, discouraged and depressed. Then they blame their exercise programs for how badly they feel.

Please don't make this mistake. To achieve your Body Shaping goals, your diet must satisfy your mouth as well as your muscles. And it's got to be a way of eating that you can live with over the long haul. Any diet that's just part of a fitness kick is going to be just that—a "kick" that won't last, undoing all your effort. The only "diet" anyone should be on is the one he or she can stay on (and enjoy) for life.

"Dieting" is the primary reason that so many people in the United States are unsuccessful at controlling their weight. We go on diets that our bodies simply can't live with. Studies show that as many as nine out of ten people who lose weight by going on weight loss "diets" wind up gaining all or most of their weight back within just a few years. Many wind up even heavier, in fact, because their diets have caused them to lose muscle tissue, thus lowering their metabolic rates and making it all that much easier for their pounds to return.

Don't let it happen to you. The best "diet" you can be on is the one that gives you all the nutrients you need plus all the pleasure you need. Anything less is going to be only a temporary detour that could have you feeling like a failure when you quit it. Worse yet, an inadequate diet is likely to seriously compromise your exercise efforts along the way, possibly even turning what should be a healthful activity into an unhealthful one. So diet is a fundamental component of any successful exercise program.

EATING HABITS THAT WORK *WITH* YOUR BODY

Few people realize that exercise exacts metabolic "costs" on the body that must be repaid in the form of ample nutrition if any appreciable "rewards" are to be won. These rewards are what's known as the training effect—the greater strength, firmness, energy and stamina that exercise imbues. But none of these benefits can accrue if there's not the investment of a sound diet behind them. Muscles cannot recover and restructure themselves from the demands exercise puts upon them, nor can the heart, lungs and any of the body's other vital systems respond by becoming stronger and more efficient as they should. The body can't even burn fat as it should in the face of inadequate nutrition and will turn to burning muscle and eventually even vital organ tissue if adequate nourishment is not on call.

No, an exercise program without the right diet is like trying to run your car without sufficient fuel or oil: Sooner or later you're going to break down or, at best, just plain run out of gas. You must learn to view food not as your enemy in your Body Shaping efforts but rather as your ally, and a very important one. You might even think about putting a sign to this effect on your refrigerator door: "Food is my friend: It will help me, not hinder me, in achieving my fitness goals." No meal skipping, extended fasts, compulsive calorie counting, fad diets or guilt-driven binges allowed.

WHAT WORKS—AND WHY

Sounds great, you say, but you still have your doubts? "No pain, no gain" is a concept that needs to be applied to the kitchen as much as the gym?

The sooner you can divorce yourself from that counterproductive thinking, the closer you'll be to achieving your Body Shaping goals. And to help you make that divorce, it might be helpful for you to get a picture of how food and exercise actually "get it together" right down on a cellular level. The process is known in scientific jargon as *supercompensation,* and it's what "getting in shape" is biochemically all about. Supercompensation is your body's way of planning ahead, in a sense, for a progression in your fitness efforts. After a workout, your body not only wants to rest; it wants to replace the energy supplies that the workout has used up. But it also goes one step further. It wants to replace those depleted energy supplies plus store away additional supplies, so you will be able to do even more work the next time.

Supercompensation is your ticket to making progress in your fitness efforts. But you need food to build your new body. So once you begin your Body Shaping workouts, don't be too restrictive in your diet, thinking that perhaps you'll be speeding your

progress. You won't—and you could even impede your progress by causing your body to cannibalize the very muscle you're trying to build.

Even if you have excess fat that you'd like to lose, you need to take in enough energy to properly fuel the exercise that's going to be most effective in burning off that fat. Without an adequate diet, your workouts simply aren't going to work as well as they could. You're not going to have the energy to pursue your workouts full-steam, and the work that you do manage is not going to be optimally effective in bringing about the changes you desire, because you're simply not going to have the "building blocks" in the way of nutrients that your body needs to produce them.

Sure, you can lose pounds—and lots of them—very quickly by starving yourself, but you'll also be losing muscle tissue and hence lowering your body's metabolic (calorie-burning) rate, the result being that you'll be that much more susceptible to putting those pounds back on, and then some, in the future. This muscle loss will occur, moreover, even if you work out, so don't think that exercise is going to afford you any sort of magical protection. You must give exercise its required fuels for it to make the bodily changes that are going to protect you against obesity. To exercise without giving your body these required fuels, as I mentioned earlier, is just adding one stress to another almost as blatantly as if you were to try to run your car without any gas.

To sum up: The Body Shaping Diet Plan is based not on counting calories but on choosing a wide variety of the right kinds of foods, in the right amounts, and eating at the right time of day. The best selections are high in complex carbohydrates and fiber, adequate (but not excessively high) in protein and low in fat, cholesterol, salt, alcohol and caffeine. The plan is based on four easy-to-follow Body Shaping Diet Principles.

BODY SHAPING DIET PRINCIPLE #1: LIMIT, BUT DO NOT ELIMINATE, DIETARY FAT

Dietary fat has been on just about everyone's nutritional chopping block these days, and for some legitimate reasons. Fat is calorically denser than protein or carbohydrates. (A single gram contains nine calories, while a gram of protein or carbohydrates contains only about four.) Also, diets high in fat—and saturated fat especially—appear to be a risk factor for obesity, heart disease, high blood pressure, stroke, diabetes and even some forms of cancer.

When it comes to Body Shaping, fat has two other important drawbacks. First of all, a high-fat diet leaves you feeling too sluggish to do your Body Shaping aerobic and toning exercises. What's more, dietary fat has a pronounced tendency to become body fat

once consumed. That's true of saturated fat especially, the kind in fatty meats, full-fat dairy products, palm and coconut oils and, yes, even margarine. Maybe that's because saturated fat is chemically very similar to body fat in the first place, so it requires very little metabolic energy (only about one-seventh as much as carbohydrates or protein) before converting to body fat once through the stomach.

So willing is saturated fat to become body fat, in fact, that the fat it produces often doesn't even get much beyond the stomach. Studies show that diets high in saturated fat tend to produce body fat in the area of the abdomen more so than anywhere else—a Body Shaper's no-no for sure. This does not mean that fat must be eliminated from the diet totally, however: It needs simply to be reduced. The body needs some fat to assimilate fat-soluble vitamins and for the manufacture of cell walls plus certain essential enzymes and hormones. Fat also helps make food both more satisfying and more filling.

Research now leaves no doubt that a high-fat diet is more likely to produce weight gain than a low-fat diet, even though the high-fat diet may be substantially lower in calories. Says Peter Vash, M.D., assistant clinical professor of medicine at the University of California, Los Angeles: "We need to start thinking of the fat we eat as the fat we wear."

That being the case, try to limit

your intake of dietary fat to no more than about 25 percent of your daily caloric intake. I know that's one of those numbers that can be very hard to translate to the real world, but you can start simply by cutting down on the most obvious no-no's such as butter, fried foods, rich sauces, hamburgers and hot dogs, full-fat salad dressings, eggs, cheese, mayonnaise and rich desserts. Also, try to choose unsaturated and monounsaturated fats over saturated fat whenever possible. This means using oils such as olive (the best), canola, peanut, safflower, sunflower and corn and being very selective in your use of margarine, butter and lard. Calorically, saturated and unsaturated fats are equal. But unsaturated fat is less brutal to your arteries.

The chart below gives a quick and easy guide to help you keep the fat in your diet at levels conducive to Body Shaping.

BODY SHAPING DIET PRINCIPLE #2: SELECT PROTEINS LOW IN FAT

You've probably heard that serious bodybuilders really go to town on protein. So where does protein fit into your Body Shaping Diet?

Protein provides the basic building blocks for cellular muscular repair and development. While carbohydrates supply energy for muscular exertion—performing your Body Shaping workouts and fat-burning aerobic exercises—protein enables your muscles to respond to this exertion by getting firmer and stronger. This is why your need for protein increases the more you put your muscles to work. Exercise causes muscles to undergo a type of intricate cellular breakdown that only protein can repair (and build upon).

If you're going to be working out regularly doing the program I recommend, you should be getting approximately ½ to ¾ gram of protein daily for every pound you weigh—60 to 90 grams, for example, if you weigh 120 pounds. Just be careful when getting your protein not to get a lot of fat. A hamburger patty, for example, can be as high as 60 percent fat, most hard cheeses about 70 percent and a hot dog a whopping 80 percent. Even a

---

THE BODY SHAPING FAT ALLOWANCE GUIDE

To improve your fat-to-muscle ratio, you don't have to swear off every last smidgen of dietary fat. Just keep fat intake to about 25 percent of total calories. This handy guide to daily fat and calorie intake will help.

Weight (pounds)	Calories	Fat (grams)
110	1300	36
120	1400	39
130	1600	44
140	1700	47
150	1800	50
160	1900	53
170	2000	56
180	2200	61

seemingly "lean" T-bone or sirloin steak can be in the neighborhood of 50 to 60 percent fat, so choose your protein carefully. Your best sources are lean meats, poultry, fish, low-fat dairy products, whole-grain cereals and breads, beans and nuts.

BODY SHAPING DIET PRINCIPLE #3: SAY YES TO CARBOHYDRATES

As you shave the fat from your menu, you should consume more calories from carbohydrates—bagels, pasta, cereals, breads, potatoes, rice, beans, fruits and vegetables. Carbohydrates are the highest-energy and, in many ways, the most healthful types of food you can eat. That may surprise you, considering the bad reputation carbohydrates were given by certain fad diets a few years back, but that's exactly what those diets were—fads that helped people lose weight only by also helping them to lose health. The diets were totally out of nutritional balance, which is precisely why so many people "fell down" on them.

So forget the notion that carbohydrates are fattening. The truth is, carbs are an exerciser's dream come true, and especially if eaten in their natural, "complex" forms. (Potato chips and candy bars don't count.) We now know that carbohydrate foods are the absolutely best foods for controlling weight, because they're without a doubt the best for supplying energy! And the more energy you have, the

more inclined—as well as the more capable—you're going to be to get good, high-quality workouts.

Carbohydrates are unique—they "rev up" your body's metabolic rate even as you're just resting, and once you begin to exercise, carbohydrates really begin to kick into gear. They are without a doubt your body's absolutely best source of energy for maximal physical and mental exertion.

A good portion of this body-revving ability of carbohydrates is known scientifically as the thermal effect of food (TEF for short). And over the long haul, this effect can be quite substantial. Eat 100 calories from fat, for example, and only 3 of those calories go toward stepping up your metabolism. But eat 100 calories from carbohydrates, and bingo—*23 calories* immediately go toward fueling your body's metabolic rate.

What this means, in essence, is that nearly one-quarter of the calories consumed as carbohydrates are "free," because they're being used to give you energy. Begin to exercise with carbohydrates in your system, moreover, and if you exercise with any degree of vigor, you create a metabolic bonfire.

No wonder, then, that carbohydrates are the preferred fuel for most competitive athletes regardless of their sport—bodybuilders and marathon runners alike. Carbohydrates make you feel most like exercising in the first place, they provide the best fuel for that exercise as it's actually in progress, and they do the best job of replenishing muscles with the energy supplies (glycogen) that exercise uses up.

By the way, carbohydrates do their absolutely best job of replacing muscle glycogen if eaten within 15 minutes of exercise. So keep that in mind in planning your workouts. A quick snack such as a piece of fresh fruit, a bagel or a high-carbohydrate sport drink can really "hit the spot" in helping your workouts to produce their optimal effects.

BODY SHAPING DIET PRINCIPLE #4: MAKE FRIENDS WITH FIBER

You may think of fiber as the key to keeping your digestive system in shape. (It is.) But fiber can affect the "shape" of your body as well. As goes your digestion, you see, so goes your body's uptake—or excretion—of dietary fat. Get enough fiber in your diet, and you help "sweep" dietary fat through your intestines before it has a chance to be fully absorbed. This spares not only your waistline, research shows, but your arteries and heart as well.

Then, too, foods high in fiber tend to take longer to digest than nonfibrous foods (a weight control plus), partly because they absorb a lot of water once in the stomach. So they fill you "up" without filling you "out." Add

the fact that the best sources of fiber are foods also rich in high-energy carbohydrates (grains, potatoes, beans), and you can see why fiber definitely belongs in your Body Shaping Diet Plan. You should try to get between 20 and 30 grams a day. That's roughly twice the amount the average American routinely consumes.

Foods highest in fiber, ranked from highest to lowest, include:

Bran (per two tablespoons)
Corn bran (7.9 grams)
Wheat bran (3.0 grams)
Rice bran (2.3 grams)
Oat bran (1.8 grams)

Cereals
Fiber One (General Mills)—½ cup (13 grams)
Fruit & Fitness (Health Valley)—¾ cup (11 grams)
All-Bran (Kellogg's)—⅓ cup (10 grams)
100% Bran (Nabisco)—½ cup (10 grams)
Raisin Bran (Post)—¾ cup (6 grams)
Ralston—¾ cup (6 grams)
Bran Flakes (Kellogg's)—⅔ cup (5 grams)
Fruit & Fibre (Post)—⅔ cup (5 grams)
Fruitful Bran (Kellogg's)—⅔ cup (5 grams)
Raisin Bran (Kellogg's)—¾ cup (5 grams)
Oatmeal—¾ cup (3.9 grams)

Grains, Legumes and Fruits

Barley, pearled, cooked—½ cup (12.3 grams)

Blackberries—1 cup (7.2 grams)

Chick-peas—½ cup (7.0 grams)

Kidney beans—½ cup (6.9 grams)

Lima beans—½ cup (6.8 grams)

Raspberries—1 cup (6.0 grams)

Figs, dried—3 figs (5.2 grams)

Lentils, cooked—½ cup (5.2 grams)

Succotash—½ cup (5.2 grams)

Currants, dried—½ cup (4.9 grams)

Navy beans, cooked—½ cup (4.9 grams)

The foods listed are by no means the only good sources of fiber. Other fresh fruits, vegetables, whole-grain rice and breads and pastas made from whole-grain flours contain approximately two to four grams of fiber per serving.

The ideal Body Shaping Diet Plan includes a wide variety of fiber-rich foods. When planning meals, combine several in one meal or recipe.

PUTTING THE BODY SHAPING DIET PRINCIPLES INTO PRACTICE

You won't have to look far to find the kinds of foods that best enable you to trim your trouble spots and erase your fat zones. A couple of years ago, the U.S. Department of Agriculture (USDA) deep-sixed the old basic four food groups we all learned about back in elementary school. In their place,

nutrition experts came up with the Food Pyramid. In this revolutionary new eating scheme, grains form the base of the pyramid, followed by vegetables and fruits, then dairy and meat products. Fats, oils and sweets appear in the smallest, uppermost area.

When it comes to figure control, the Food Pyramid is right on. So I've built the Body Shaping Diet around the number of servings for each food that are recommended for women. The best part about the Body Shaping plan is that you don't have to put every calorie you eat under a microscope. To build your Food Pyramid, follow these tips. (The higher number of servings is for active women; all others should consume the lower number of servings. Also, bigger portions, such as a cup of pasta, count as two servings.)

BREAD, CEREAL, RICE AND PASTA
6 to 9 servings

Grains are among the most nutritious foods you can find. As the nutrient storehouses of wheat, oats, rice, millet, rye and barley, grains are rich in vitamins and minerals. But what makes them perfect for a Body Shaping program is that they provide the greatest amount of energy, consisting of 70 to 85 percent carbohydrates, 5 to 10 percent protein, plus fiber. No wonder that grains (along with beans and legumes) serve as a staple for so many cultures.

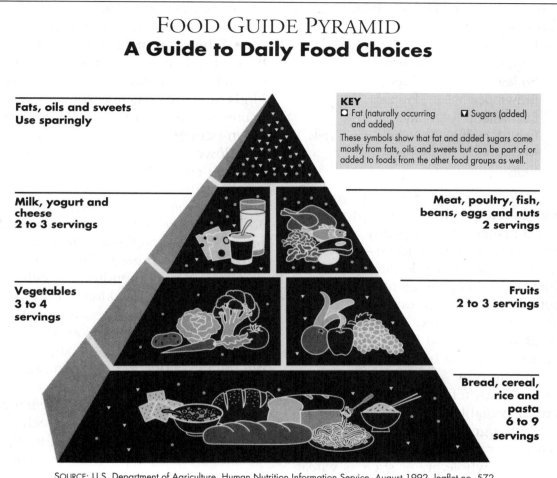

FOOD GUIDE PYRAMID
A Guide to Daily Food Choices

**Fats, oils and sweets
Use sparingly**

KEY
☐ Fat (naturally occurring and added)   ☑ Sugars (added)

These symbols show that fat and added sugars come mostly from fats, oils and sweets but can be part of or added to foods from the other food groups as well.

**Milk, yogurt and cheese
2 to 3 servings**

**Meat, poultry, fish, beans, eggs and nuts
2 servings**

**Vegetables
3 to 4 servings**

**Fruits
2 to 3 servings**

**Bread, cereal, rice and pasta
6 to 9 servings**

SOURCE: U.S. Department of Agriculture, Human Nutrition Information Service, August 1992, leaflet no. 572.

I highly recommend grain foods for breakfast and lunch. One slice of bread, ½ cup of cooked rice or pasta, ½ cup of cooked cereal and one ounce of ready-to-eat cereal each count as a serving.

To fulfill your quota of these valuable complex carbohydrates, think beyond the popular white rice and white flour baked goods. Choose from whole-grain products, and go for variety. Also, beware of baked goods. Corn bread, muffins and pancakes made with whole grains and little fat are fine. Avoid fat-enhanced baked goods such as biscuits, bread stuffing and high-fat quick breads. Read labels of pastries, taco shells, pancake mixes and so forth for fat content. Stay away from corn chips, doughnuts, potato chips, high-fat crackers, cookies, cakes and sweet rolls.

Look for:

Bagels	Pasta
Barley	Popcorn
Brown rice	Pretzels
Buckwheat	Rye
English muffins	Whole-grain rolls,
Millet	breads
Oats	

If time permits, try making your own breads. With the new automatic bread makers, it's not nearly as time-consuming as it used to be—the machines do all the work. Simply add the flour and other ingredients, push a button, and go work out while the bread rises and bakes. If your workout program leaves you little time for activities like bread baking, you can compromise by searching out the most natural, least refined commercial loaves available.

With a grain grinder, you can even make your own highly nutritious cereals from whole grains such as wheat, oats, barley, brown rice, millet and rye—much richer in nutrients than processed cereals that have been sitting on the shelves for months.

VEGETABLES
3 to 4 servings

When you follow the Food Pyramid plan, vegetables aren't after-thoughts—they're mainstays. (One cup of raw vegetables or ½ cup of cooked equals one serving.) Here are some tips for working them into your menu.

• When you make a salad, think beyond iceberg lettuce, tomatoes and cucumbers. Use two or three different kinds of greens (such as spinach, romaine and kohlrabi). Then add celery, green peppers, red onions, broccoli, cauliflower, carrots—any raw vegetables you enjoy.

• To further liven up salads and work in some foods from the grains and legumes group, toss some cooked pasta (such as rotelle or rotini), peas or beans on your greens. In this way, you can consume hundreds of satisfying calories while taking in only 20 grams of fat. (You may even want to consider making a salad your entrée.)

• Keep a sealed plastic bag or two full of raw, cut-up veggies handy in your crisper: broccoli, carrots, zucchini, cauliflower, asparagus, green or red peppers, pea pods, fresh green beans, chick-peas, mushrooms, turnips and tomatoes. These can make great snacks, too, far superior to your standard pretzels and chips.

• Experiment with vegetables that are new to you. With so much variety to choose from, replacing fatty foods with vegetables should be a delight. I'd recommend the following, especially when they're in season.

Artichokes	Beets
Asparagus	Bok choy
Bamboo shoots	Broccoli
Beet greens	Brussels sprouts

Cabbage
  (red, white)
Carrots
Cauliflower
Collards
Corn
Cucumbers
Daikon
  radishes
Dandelion
Eggplant
Endive
Escarole
Garden beans
  (green, string,
  yellow)
Jícama
Kale
Kohlrabi
Leeks
Lettuce (Boston,
  Bibb, butter-
  head, green
  leaf, red leaf,
  romaine)

Mushrooms
Mustard greens
Okra
Onions
  (green, red,
  white, yellow;
  shallots)
Peppers
  (green, red,
  yellow)
Plantains
Potatoes
Pumpkin
Radishes
Rutabaga
Spinach
Sprouts
Squash
  (all varieties)
Sweet potatoes
Tomatoes
Turnip greens
Turnips

FRUITS
2 to 3 servings

Fruit is a great way to start the day—it quenches your thirst while it fills you up, and whole or pureed fruit is a reliable source of fiber.

On the Food Pyramid, one medium whole fruit, ½ cup of fresh or canned fruit, ¼ cup of dried fruit or six ounces of juice constitutes one serving. But whenever you can, I urge you to go

for the whole fruit (preferably locally grown and naturally ripened produce). It's more satisfying. A study conducted at the Royal Infirmary in Bristol, England, for example, timed individuals as they consumed whole apples, applesauce or apple juice. On the average, it took 17 minutes to eat the apple, compared with 6 minutes to eat the applesauce and 1½ minutes to drink the juice. Eating the whole fruit was more satisfying (and blood sugar and insulin levels were more stable) than eating applesauce or drinking juice. (Another reason why a piece of fruit makes a great pre-workout snack.)

If you rely on canned fruit for convenience, drain off the sugary syrup. (Or buy varieties canned in natural juice.)

Choose from this wide variety of fruit.

Apples
Apricots
Avocados
Bananas
Berries
  (blackberries,
  blueberries,
  cranberries,
  raspberries)
Cherries
Dates
Figs
Grapefruit
Grapes
Guavas
Kiwifruit

Kumquats
Mangoes
Melons
  (cantaloupe,
  casaba,
  Crenshaw,
  honeydew,
  muskmelon,
  Persian melon,
  watermelon)
Nectarines
Oranges
  (mandarin,
  regular)
Papayas
Passion fruit

Peaches
Pears
Persimmons
Pineapple
Plums
Pomegranates
Prickly pears

Prunes
Quince
Raisins
Rhubarb
Tangelos
Tangerines

Wash fruits just before serving. Otherwise, moisture leaches out valuable nutrients and speeds decay. Store in a paper bag in the crisper of the fridge to maintain freshness.

MILK, YOGURT AND CHEESE
2 to 3 servings

Eight ounces of low-fat milk, one cup of yogurt or 1½ to 2 ounces of cheese equals one serving. (Always look for reduced-fat or nonfat cheese.) Women who are breastfeeding need three servings a day.

The following supply fewer than five grams of fat per serving and less than 30 percent of calories from fat.

Buttermilk—1 cup
Low-fat (1 percent) cottage
   cheese—½ cup
Low-fat (1 percent) milk—1 cup
Low-fat yogurt—1 cup
Nonfat milk—1 cup
Nonfat yogurt—1 cup

A fair number of adults (and some children) cannot tolerate large amounts of lactose, a natural sugar found in milk. If lactose is a problem for you, try buttermilk, acidophilus milk or lactose-reduced milk (or drink only small quantities).

MEAT, POULTRY, FISH, BEANS, EGGS AND NUTS
2 servings

Active women should consume a total of six ounces of meat a day; others, five ounces. Or you can substitute plant sources of protein part of the time. The trick to getting protein, remember, is to avoid consuming a lot of fat and cholesterol. Also, too much protein has been indicted as a health hazard. Besides, meat, poultry and fish contain no fiber or complex carbohydrates, both of which are essential if your Body Shaping program is to work. So to fulfill your daily quota of this food group, concentrate on foods rich in high-quality protein such as lean meats, poultry, beans and—my favorite—fish (as well as the low-fat dairy products mentioned earlier).

The USDA includes nuts in this category. While fresh raw nuts (and seeds) are an excellent source of protein, fiber, vitamins and minerals, I prefer to think of them as either vegetables (because of their carbohydrate content) or oils (because of their high fat content). As with olive oil, nuts and seeds (including peanut butter) can be part of the Body Shaping Diet Plan, as long as they're not abused.

On the Body Shaping program, I strongly advise that you save your meat, poultry and fish allotment for the evening meal, concentrating on the energy-boosting carbohydrates earlier in the day.

The following foods—all of which derive less than 30 percent of their calories from fat and supply fewer than five grams of fat per serving—can help you do just that.

Beef, Pork, Veal and Game (per three-ounce serving)
Eye round roast, lean only
Pheasant
Pork tenderloin
Top round steak, lean only
Veal
Venison

Poultry (per three-ounce serving)
Chicken breast
Turkey, white meat

Fish (per three-ounce serving)

A few years back, fish and seafood soared in popularity in the wake of news that the omega-3 fatty acids they contain may benefit the heart. Coupled with reports that not all types of seafood contain as much cholesterol as was previously thought, many people eat fish up to three times a week or more. Don't sabotage these low-fat sources of protein by deep-frying them or using high-fat sauces, though. Broiling (with little or no oil or butter), baking, poaching and steaming are your best bets.

Bass	Grouper
Cod	Haddock
Flounder	Halibut
Mahimahi	Sole
Monkfish	Swordfish
Perch	Trout
Pike	Tuna (albacore or
Pollock	chunk light)
Shark	Turbot
Snapper	Whitefish

Shellfish (per three-ounce serving)

Clams	Mussels
Crab	Scallops
Lobster	Shrimp

Beans (per ½-cup serving)

Beans, peas and legumes supply just a smidgen of fat and plenty of fiber and complex carbohydrates. Nutrient-rich, inexpensive sources of protein, beans, peas and legumes are a low-fat alternative to meat and poultry, especially when combined with grains. You can't go wrong with this list.

Adzuki beans	Lima beans
Black beans	Navy beans
Black-eyed	Pink beans
peas	Pinto beans
Broad beans	Soybeans (in-
Chick-peas	cluding soybean
(garbanzos)	grits, tempeh,
Fava beans	tofu)
Kidney beans	Split peas
Lentils	Whole dried peas

Not all beans produce gas, and not all individuals are affected. To disperse 90 percent of the gas-forming sugars in beans before they hit your digestive tract, USDA researchers say: Rinse beans thoroughly, then presoak for four hours. Discard soaking water, cover with fresh water, and cook until soft.

Eggs

It's okay to eat a whole egg or two once in a while. But people who are watching their fat and cholesterol intake can avail themselves of the following, especially when recipes call for eggs.

Egg substitute, frozen—¼ cup
Egg substitute, liquid—¼ cup
Egg whites (from 1 large egg)

If you're watching your sodium intake, check labels on egg substitutes to find one that works for you.

FATS, OILS AND SWEETS
use sparingly

These appear in the tiny peak of the Food Pyramid not because they're tops. Far from it. Fats are the nemesis of so many. Try to avoid obviously high sources of fat (such as butter) and sugar (such as candy and soft drinks). Of the liquid vegetable oils to choose from, I favor olive oil—it's highest in monounsaturated fat and linked to favorable cholesterol levels *when eaten in moderation.* Also, when it comes to heart health, research suggests that margarine is not necessarily better than butter.

Watch out, too, for foods laced with shortening or sweeteners.

Small amounts of liquid vegetable fat—especially olive oil or canola oil—are all you need to fulfill your daily requirements for fat. Eliminate snack foods cooked in oil, high-fat sauces, dressings and dips.

Speaking of salad dressing: Research in Cornell University's Division of Nutritional Sciences cited salad dressing as the single greatest source of fat in the average woman's diet. The typical weight-conscious woman, trying to live on salads, consumes about 5.2 grams of fat a day (or 47 calories' worth) from salad dressing alone. That may not seem like very much. But over the course of a year, that adds up to over 17,000 calories—enough to pack on five pounds of fat. To negate the extra fat calories, you'd need to walk 170 miles. I suggest a simple vinaigrette, with a modicum of fat: either vinegar and a little olive oil or a tad of olive oil, lemon juice and black pepper.

Here are some other helpful ways for you to replace common sources of dietary fat.

• Use apple butter or other fruit spreads instead of butter or margarine on bagels, toast, waffles or crackers.

• If you must use margarine, stick with products with the lowest saturated fat content you can find.

• When you sauté, stir-fry or bake, use nonstick vegetable spray instead of butter, lard or shortening.

The number of fat-free products has increased astronomically over the past few years, and a number of nonfat (or low-fat) substitutes are available: evaporated skim milk, fat-free cream cheese, nonfat or low-fat cottage cheese and fat-free or reduced-fat cheeses instead of whole milk or cream, regular cream cheese and other full-fat cheeses, nonfat or low-fat yogurt (frozen or regular) and fat-free or reduced-calorie mayonnaise. But in my experience, this can sometimes backfire: Knowing the products are low in fat, some people have a tendency to eat *more*.

The other drawback is that the reconstituted versions of the real thing lack fat-soluble nutrients and possibly other undiscovered nutrients. (Scientists are still discovering new vitamins and minerals that, up until now, were not thought to be important to human health.) To be sure you're getting an adequate supply of everything you need, I feel strongly that the diet should include foods that are as close as possible to their natural state—and that includes fat. I advise my clients to eat the real thing, but sparingly, rather than loading up on the reformulated versions.

One more thing: Don't rely too heavily on artificial sweeteners. An ongoing study of more than 78,000 women between the ages of 50 and 69, conducted by the American Cancer Society, found that over the course of one year, women who use artificial sweeteners are more likely to gain weight than nonusers. One study in England suggests that artificial sweeteners may *increase* feelings of hunger. The theory is that even though a diet soda may not contain sugar, evidently the brain interprets all sweetness equally and triggers changes in blood sugar that mimic a reaction to sugar.

Now that you've gotten the basics under your belt, here are a few more Body Shaping guidelines that will speed you toward your goal.

KEEP IT SIMPLE

When it comes to preparing food for Body Shaping, less is better. Don't overcook vegetables and/or obliterate otherwise healthful foods with high-fat cooking techniques such as deep-frying or sautéing in gobs of lard or butter. It's been my own experience that foods eaten as close as possible to their natural state provide maximum nutrition and taste with minimum fuss.

So do yourself a favor: Leave the time-consuming (and calorie-adding) gourmet cooking techniques to French chefs. Try to appreciate foods for what they are as opposed to what they become once adulterated by some high-fat garnish or sauce, and you'll be that much ahead of the game. Is it really necessary, for example, to whip up the old hollandaise in order to enjoy a serving of fresh broccoli? Or to get out the butter to enjoy a sweet and juicy ear of corn? Or to sabotage an otherwise low-fat turkey or chicken sandwich with a couple of hundred calories' worth of mayonnaise?

THINK MINI-MEALS

I advise people to eat at least three times a day. That's right—no meal skipping and especially no fasting allowed.

Studies show that skipping meals is counterproductive to weight control because it slows down fat burning by slowing down the metabolism. Worse yet, it sets up the likelihood of another classic eating blunder—the "binge" that treats fat cells to a smorgasbord. Overeating causes the pancreas to put out proportionately more insulin than would be called upon by a normal-size meal, the result being that fat cells become more inclined to store calories instead of letting them be used by the body for energy. Add the tendency to do nothing more physical than collapse on the couch that's the normal consequence of a large meal, and you can see why large, infrequent meals and large bodies tend to go hand in hand. One study of obese people found that even among those who ate no more calories than normal-weight individuals, fully 80 percent tended to skip meals, then gorge.

For people who exercise, ignoring the need to eat can double-sabotage your Body Shaping efforts. When you skip meals, you essentially ask your body to run on empty, and how well can you perform your everyday tasks (much less your workouts) in that state? Not well, I assure you. Worse yet, skipping meals deprives your muscles of optimal "re-feeding" supplies— hence the need for pre-exercise snacks, as mentioned in the discussion of carbohydrates earlier in this chapter.

Keep that in mind the next time

you're feeling "too busy" to eat. If you don't have time for a conventional meal, there's nothing wrong with a healthful snack such as a piece of fruit, a small sandwich or a container of low-fat yogurt. One recent survey of women who were successful in maintaining a normal weight found that most of them, in addition to exercising regularly, were following this frequent feeding rule. Some ate as many as five or six "mini-meals" a day.

DRINK LOTS OF WATER

To return to my automotive analogy for a moment, your body needs not just enough "gas" (nutrients and calories) to do its best work but enough water, too. This is because water not only keeps you hydrated enough to exercise with maximum efficiency, it also helps your body cool itself plus get rid of its natural waste products. To be a "lean machine," it helps to also be a "clean machine," and drinking enough water can help you do it.

Then, too, there's a cosmetic consideration. Drinking enough water can help avoid the "dry skin syndrome" that sometimes can bother women when they first begin to work out. When you exercise, you lose water not just through sweat but also through your breathing, and the losses can be substantial.

Don't get me wrong—sweating is natural and desirable. Perspiration cools the body, gets rid of waste products and cleanses the pores. But it does deplete the body of water that must be replaced. So play it safe. Try to drink no fewer than eight eight-ounce glasses of water a day—not soda, coffee or tea. (One rule of thumb suggests a quart a day for every 50 pounds you weigh.) And don't wait until you're thirsty to drink. Your body can be short of water without your thirst letting you know about it.

EAT FOOD, NOT PILLS

I cannot overemphasize the importance of eating fresh and natural foods whenever possible. Don't let yourself be duped by the fantastic advertising claims often made for certain high-priced "health foods" and supplements. If you eat wisely from each of the Food Pyramid groups, you shouldn't need any additional supplementation other than perhaps a multiple vitamin "just to be sure." And as for "health foods," there are none better than you can make for yourself from natural foods purchased as fresh as possible from your local supermarket. Fresh-squeezed orange juice, for example: We had a friend visit our house once who didn't know what it was when we served it to her—that's how much tastier it was than the orange juice made from concentrate she had been used to.

ENJOY YOUR FOOD

With a little imagination and not a lot of work, you can make your healthy diet extremely enjoyable. And it's important that you do, because any diet you don't love is one you're going to leave. If your diet isn't giving you pleasure, it's lacking, regardless of how nutritionally complete it may be.

Important, too, is allowing yourself your favorite foods, because many times foods that you "crave" are trying to tell you something about your body's chemistry. A craving for something sweet, for example, could be a sign that your blood sugar has fallen too low. (Don't make this a habit, though.) Or a strong urge for something salty could mean that the sweat you're losing in your workouts has caused your body's sodium levels to dip. Learn to respect your body's messages once you start working out, because they're usually trying to tell you something you should hear. And when you do partake in something a little special, don't feel "guilty" about it. Erase that word from your vocabulary. If you're exercising regularly, the food will have a purpose.

RECRUIT YOUR FAMILY'S HELP

Weight problems are partly hereditary, partly environmental. Whether you realize it or not, you set the example for your children, so the healthier the lifestyle you can show them—in terms of your diet and exercise habits alike—the better for all concerned. The Body Shaping Diet Plan isn't a special, restrictive diet for just a few. Everyone can benefit from the basic Body Shaping Diet Principles, even if they're satisfied with their weight and shape. So you might want to think about encouraging your parents, spouse or children to share in the healthful and innovative changes in your eating habits. Ask them to help you shop, plan and prepare meals.

It's been my own personal experience, plus a phenomenon I've observed, that the pursuit of fitness is always most enjoyable and most effective when it's made a family affair.

Now it's time to see how the Body

Shaping Diet Principles we've discussed might actually be brought to your plate. The sample meals presented on the following pages incorporate surprisingly normal, ample and satisfying fare.

You should feel free to follow the Food Pyramid guidelines to concoct nutritious and delicious meals of your own. The more energy and creativity you can put into your efforts in the kitchen, the more success you're likely to enjoy in the gym. Good luck, and bon appétit.

SEVEN DAYS OF BODY SHAPING MENUS

What follows are sample meal plans showing the kind of simplicity and variety to strive for on the Body Shaping Diet Plan. Follow the guidelines given in the text for the portion sizes and number of servings recommended for women.

DAY ONE

Breakfast   100% fruit juice (not fruit drink)
Cooked cereal (oatmeal or Cream of Wheat) with raisins
Low-fat milk
Cantaloupe wedge with squeeze of lime juice

Lunch   Tossed salad with escarole, julienned carrots, chopped red cabbage and vinaigrette or red wine vinegar
Fusilli, rotini or other pasta with meat sauce
Whole-wheat roll or bread sticks

Dinner   Freshly cut raw vegetables (cauliflorets, green peppers, mushrooms, scallions)
Broiled haddock, perch, snapper or other fish with lemon wedge
Brown rice, cooked
Broccoli, lightly steamed
Baked acorn or butternut squash with crushed pineapple

Snacks   Low-fat vanilla yogurt topped with wheat germ
Pretzels
Seasonal fruit

(continued)

SEVEN DAYS OF BODY SHAPING MENUS — CONTINUED

DAY TWO

Breakfast   One whole fresh grapefruit
Multi-grain cereal (such as Nutri-Grain)
Low-fat milk
Whole-grain toast with all-fruit spread or sugarless jam

Lunch   Turkey sandwich with whole-grain bread, Bibb lettuce, sliced
tomatoes and mustard
Tangerine or other fruit

Dinner   Stir-fried beef or pork with snow peas, red peppers, bok choy
and minced gingerroot
Brown rice
Salad with romaine lettuce, beets, red onion and lemon and
olive oil dressing
Multi-grain bread
Grilled banana topped with low-fat vanilla or strawberry yogurt

Snacks   Popcorn
Seasonal fruit

DAY THREE

Breakfast   Freshly squeezed orange juice or other fruit juice
Oatmeal with raisins or other fruit
Low-fat milk
Whole-grain English muffin with apple butter

Lunch   Turkey barley soup
Three-bean salad with chopped red onion, basil and red wine vinaigrette
Peach, nectarine or other seasonal fruit
Whole-wheat crackers

Dinner   Broiled or grilled chicken
Baked potato with parsley
Spinach or Swiss chard
Yellow squash
Whole-wheat roll

Snack   Watermelon or other melon

(continued)

Seven Days of Body Shaping Menus — Continued

DAY FOUR

Breakfast Freshly squeezed orange juice or other fruit juice
Whole-grain banana muffins (from freshly ground oats, wheat, rye, rice, millet)
Low-fat milk
Sliced fruit

Lunch Fruit juice spritzer
Vanilla yogurt with blueberries, raspberries or strawberries
One wheat bagel

Dinner Crudités (jícama, red pepper, carrots)
Broiled scallops
Coleslaw (minimum mayonnaise)
French-cut green beans sautéed with almonds
Corn bread or cornmeal muffin
Baked apple with cinnamon

Snacks Honey graham crackers
Yogurt or seasonal fruit

DAY FIVE

Breakfast Honeydew, casaba or other melon wedge
Cooked whole-grain cereal (freshly ground, if possible)
Low-fat milk

Lunch Lentil soup
Spinach salad with sliced mushrooms and red onion
Whole-wheat croutons or bread sticks
All-vegetable juice

Dinner Roast turkey or chicken
Baked sweet potato
Green or red leaf lettuce salad with lemon and olive oil dressing
Corn on the cob
Baked mashed turnips, rutabaga or parsnips
Whole-wheat roll

Snack Whole-wheat pita wedges, toasted, with low-fat Monterey Jack cheese

DAY SIX

Breakfast Pineapple-banana-orange juice
Whole-wheat pancakes topped with pureed fruit
Low-fat yogurt with Grape-Nuts or toasted wheat germ

Lunch Bean burritos in corn tortilla shells with chopped tomatoes, lettuce, onion and
jalapeño or pepperoncini peppers
Salsa
Brown rice
Kiwifruit, mango or papaya

Dinner Vegetable pasta (spaghetti squash) with Parmesan cheese
Tossed salad with Boston lettuce or endive, asparagus, cherry tomatoes and
chick-peas
Italian bread topped with sliced plum tomatoes, grated low-fat mozzarella
cheese and fresh basil, toasted
Fresh figs

Snack Oat bran crackers

DAY SEVEN

Breakfast Tropical fruit juice (not fruit drink)
Whole-grain waffles topped with berries and yogurt
Mixed fruit salad
Whole-wheat toast

Lunch Pasta salad with peas, artichoke hearts, chopped scallions and water-packed
tuna, tossed with basil, parsley, red wine vinegar or balsamic vinegar and
a few drops of olive oil
Mixed fruit cup
Pumpernickel roll

Dinner Chicken kabobs grilled with skewered vegetables
Wild rice pilaf (steamed brown and wild rice tossed with thyme or parsley)
Ice milk or frozen low-fat yogurt

Snacks Low-fat fig bars
Seasonal fruit

❖

CHAPTER 15

MAKING IT LAST

21 tips for staying in shape

Once you've sculpted your body into shape, you'll want to keep it that way. But working out can sometimes be boring. It can take time away from other things we'd rather do. And sometimes, it's just plain hard work. (That's why it's called working out.)

So I'm offering a few mental strategies for sticking with your workouts, watching what you eat and maintaining your success at reaching whatever Body Shaping goals you've achieved. (These suggestions can also help you achieve your desired shape in the first place.)

Yes, your body must ultimately do the work, but it's your mind that must generate the enthusiasm to get your body to do that work in the first place.

I find that as women mature, they're more willing to invest time in themselves.

So whether you're about to do your first Curl-Up or your millionth, you're going to need a master plan—and a master attitude, because you're bound to encounter some obstacles. Whether it be by the demands of your family, your career or simply those times when just can't quite seem to muster the get-up-and-go, your resolve is going to be tested, and you're going to need to be strong in your mind and body alike.

So here we go: 21 proven strategies for helping you to achieve your Body Shaping goals. Don't leave for the gym without them.

1. GET DRESSED

Ask most people what they think is the toughest part of working out, and they'll probably say it's lifting heavy weights, the intensity of the workout, the time it takes, the repetitive nature of most workout routines and such. And these replies are valid. But the toughest part of any workout, the most easily overlooked, in my opinion, is changing clothes!

Farfetched, you say? Don't laugh. Look at it this way: If weight training, performing aerobics or competing in sports is your full-time job, getting dressed is part of a ritual—it's automatic. You do it without much thought. But if you're taking aerobics or lifting weights to lose weight and shape up, then changing into your workout clothes becomes stressful.

To illustrate, try to recall a busy day at work that left you very tired. You were scheduled to work out and had on your "good" clothes. You probably didn't say to yourself "I'm sure glad I have to work out now." It took a lot of effort to get into gear.

So try to think *past* the nuisance of changing clothes. Chances are pretty good that once you're dressed for the part, you're halfway there.

2. FORGET THE EXCUSES

Yes, I know. Your children have the chicken pox. Your husband got home late from the office. You have a report to finish, and you can't make it to the gym. Some excuses are unavoidable. And you shouldn't make your plans so inflexible that they can't be changed. Leave room for contingencies, so you can make adjustments as needed. But try to separate the real excuses from those that are merely convenient.

3. SCHEDULE EXERCISE FIRST

On a calendar full of commitments, an activity not scheduled is the one most likely to be dropped. Schedule your exercise sessions the same way you'd schedule a business appointment. If you must skip a workout, reschedule it before the end of the week.

4. IF YOU HATE IT, TRY AGAIN

Your first try at anything—taking a step class, using a treadmill, cooking with less fat—may not necessarily be a fun-filled and satisfying experience. Stick with it. As you become more skilled, you'll enjoy it more. Almost all your "likes" are things you can do well!

5. START SLOWLY

Can't handle 10-pound weights? Try 5. Can't handle 5? Start with 2. And don't be discouraged if you stay on Level 1 for several weeks (or months). Your body needs time to adapt in order for the gains to last. Similarly, don't plan on losing more than a pound or two a week. If you're losing more than 2 pounds a week, you're probably cannibalizing muscle, not burning fat, as workout fuel.

6. PROGRESS GRADUALLY, AT YOUR OWN PACE

True, you don't want to start out with more than you can handle. But you should try to challenge yourself, to work up to more intense efforts—more weights, more reps or longer aerobic workouts—in order to progress. Let yourself plateau, and you won't see significant results.

7. JUST DO IT

Avoid saying "I'll exercise later." Face it: You probably won't.

Almost everyone procrastinates at some time or another, about one thing or another—you decide to do something, then put it off until later. *Chronic* procrastination, however, can defeat all your intentions. Skipping one or two workouts is no big deal—things happen. Let it pass. But if you find yourself skipping more days than you exercise, try to figure out *why* you're skipping your workouts.

Is the thought of facing the task at hand too overwhelming? Are you afraid it will be too difficult? Are you afraid you'll fail at what you're trying to do?

Not only does procrastinating jeopardize the success of your program, it also is stressful and lowers your self-esteem, further snuffing your motivation to stick with your program.

Serious procrastination may call for outside counseling. Most of us procrastinate mildly and can stem this tendency with a little conscious effort. Every time you hear yourself thinking "I'll do it later," do it now.

8. KEEP A WORKOUT DIARY

An exercise diary can be the most powerful motivator of all. (Several sample pages appear on pages 58 through 62.) Record how much weight and how many reps and sets you do. Keep a similar diary of what kind of aerobic activity you do, when and for how long. You may also want to note how you felt before and after your workouts—tired and sluggish at first, energized and full of zip at the end.

If you still menstruate, you might want to note the first and last days of your period, too. Many women find they do their best before or after their period, and others, during their period (although most should not schedule highly strenuous activity at this time).

9. GET A FEEL FOR EXERCISE

Pay attention to what the exercise feels like. Over time, your muscles will "remember" the way it feels to do an exercise, and you will be able to tell if it's working for you or if something is amiss. If something doesn't feel quite right to you, don't give up. Check to see if you're performing the exercise correctly.

10. IGNORE A LAPSE

If you do skip a workout, don't turn it into an extended layoff. It's an Isolated Incident, not a Sign of Permanent Failure. If you help yourself to a double-fudge sundae, don't go on a major binge. Sticking to it *over the long haul* is what's going to bring you success. So don't get thrown off track by every little bump in the road.

11. FORGET ABOUT BEING PERFECT

In an article in *Fitness Management,* Barbara Brehm, Ed.D., associate professor of exercise and sports studies at Smith College in Northampton, Massachusetts, points out that some people feel that if they can't be the best-looking body at the pool or in the weight room, there's no sense in going at all.

Others, according to Dr. Brehm, believe that they have to do something perfectly or not do it at all. Believing that you have to adhere to a program perfectly is irrational. Perfection in any pursuit is impossible. Sometimes you just can't help missing a workout or eating more than you should (or too much of the wrong food). But it makes no sense to add insult to injury by beating yourself up when these times occur. Just know that you're doing your best and approach your next workout with even more enthusiasm and resolve.

Don't set yourself up for disappointment. Come up with an exercise schedule that's realistic for you and stick to it as best you can.

12. HALF A WORKOUT IS BETTER THAN NONE

Again, you don't have to do something perfectly or not do it at all. Flexibility is as important mentally as it is physically.

13. GIVE IT SIX WEEKS

Studies show that it typically takes approximately six to eight weeks to get hooked on exercise—to reach the point where you truly love what you're doing and feel great satisfaction from the effort.

Coincidentally, it's at this point that you'll begin to feel stronger. Your body will function better, you'll feel better mentally, and you'll gain confidence. You'll like what you see and want more. When this happens, many people shift into high gear, adjusting their schedules to make even more time to work out, even making it the focal point of their day. When that happens, you know you've passed the "sticking point."

14. TRY A VARIETY OF EXERCISES

The fastest way to get stale is to do the same thing day after day. If you always head for the treadmill, use an exercise bicycle or slideboard instead. If you always play racquetball with the same person, try to find a new partner or two.

15. DON'T OBSESS OVER FOOD

Try to avoid thinking in terms of "good" foods or "bad" foods. Instead, think "variety" when following the Body Shaping Diet Plan. Don't focus on one type of food—more carbohydrates or less fat—and ignore the big picture. Make it a point to add new and interesting foods to your menu, so you don't feel bored and deprived.

Also, don't tell friends you're on a "diet." Just tell them you're "eating healthier."

16. BANISH NEGATIVE THOUGHTS AND FEELINGS

Negative beliefs—that you can't possibly lose all that weight or that you'll never have a flat abdomen—are powerful but imaginary obstacles. But they're harder to shake than the weight itself, especially if you've held the negative concept for years. But negative beliefs can be changed, and changed very quickly, if you refuse to let them invade your thoughts. This is tough to do at first, but persevere. (It gets easier.)

17. TALK POSITIVE SELF-TALK

Research shows that affirmations— simple, positive statements that reflect your beliefs and intents—are powerful ways to keep on track or change for the better.

18. SAY "YES, I CAN"

You may surprise yourself—you can probably do more than you think you can. Think positively, and you'll get positive results. The goal is to focus on the process of making positive changes and on improvement, not on perfection.

19. BELIEVE IN YOURSELF

If you don't believe you can succeed, who will? Be your own best friend. You can do whatever you set out to do. But you have to *want* it. And you have to believe in your ability to make it happen.

The great thing about exercise is that it's not just an end in itself—it's a means of helping you to achieve *other* things in life.

20. REWARD YOURSELF

Many women I've worked with find it helpful to give themselves some kind of reward. You don't necessarily have to go out and buy something expensive for yourself. Take a bubble bath. Read a few chapters from a spellbinding novel. Or just congratulate yourself for doing what you set out to do during the day. The most motivating reinforcement is internally generated. It's okay to give yourself a pat on the back.

21. KEEP AN EYE ON THE FUTURE

By "the future," I mean the great new body you're going to have and the dynamic new attitude that's going to go with it. Don't give a second thought to failed attempts to exercise or lose weight that you may have experienced in the past. They're over, you've learned by them, and now you're wiser and more ready than ever to do things right. Sometimes it takes a few stumbles before you can learn to walk, after all.

Finally, I'd like to say that looking better is only one reward of successful Body Shaping. There are many hidden rewards of exercise that are hard to put into words.

If I had to list the bonuses, I'd say the list includes:

- Better concentration.
- Self-confidence.
- Unity between mind and body.
- Improved outlook.
- Persistence.
- Dedication.
- Self-reliance.

All those qualities make you more attractive, to yourself and others. Good luck!

ABOUT THE AUTHORS

Michael Yessis, Ph.D., is president of Sports Training, Inc., in Escondido, California, where he specializes in training athletes and producing sports- and fitness-related equipment, videos and publications. He's acted as consultant to several Olympic and professional sports teams, including the Los Angeles Rams, the Los Angeles Raiders and the U.S. men's volleyball team, among others.

Dr. Yessis is also professor emeritus at California State University, Fullerton, and frequently lectures on sports conditioning and biomechanics. He invented the glute-ham developer, the only machine that isolates and develops the lower back muscles through a full range of motion.

Dr. Yessis is a columnist for *Muscle and Fitness* magazine, editor of *Fitness and Sports Review International* and associate editor of the *National Strength and Conditioning Association Journal*. Previous books include *Kinesiology of Exercise*.

Porter Shimer is a journalist specializing in health and fitness. His articles have appeared in *Prevention, Men's Health, Muscle and Health* and *Healthy Woman* magazines, among others. His previous books include *Fitness through Pleasure* and *Fitness without Exercise* with Bryant A. Stamford, Ph.D.

INDEX